THE
PONY EXPRESS

MILESTONES
IN AMERICAN HISTORY

THE ACQUISITION OF FLORIDA

THE ALAMO

ALEXANDER GRAHAM BELL
AND THE TELEPHONE

THE ATTACK ON PEARL HARBOR

THE CALIFORNIA GOLD RUSH

THE CIVIL RIGHTS ACT OF 1964

THE DONNER PARTY

THE ELECTRIC LIGHT

THE EMANCIPATION PROCLAMATION

THE ERIE CANAL

THE LOUISIANA PURCHASE

MANIFEST DESTINY

THE MONROE DOCTRINE

THE OREGON TRAIL

THE OUTBREAK OF THE CIVIL WAR

THE PONY EXPRESS

THE PROHIBITION ERA

THE ROBBER BARONS AND THE
SHERMAN ANTITRUST ACT

THE SINKING OF THE USS *MAINE*

SPUTNIK/EXPLORER I

THE STOCK MARKET CRASH OF 1929

THE TRANSCONTINENTAL RAILROAD

THE TREATY OF PARIS

THE WRIGHT BROTHERS

MILESTONES
IN AMERICAN HISTORY

THE PONY EXPRESS

BRINGING MAIL TO THE AMERICAN WEST

TIM MCNEESE

CHELSEA HOUSE
PUBLISHERS
An imprint of Infobase Publishing

The Pony Express

Chelsea House
An imprint of Infobase Publishing
132 West 31st Street
New York NY 10001

Library of Congress Cataloging-in-Publication Data
McNeese, Tim.
  The Pony Express : bringing mail to the American West / Tim McNeese.
      p. cm. — (Milestones in American history)
  Includes bibliographical references and index.
  ISBN 978-1-60413-028-7 (hbk.)
  1. Pony express—History—Juvenile literature. 2. Postal service—United States—History—19th century—Juvenile literature. I. Title. II. Series.
  HE6375.P65M237 2009
  383'.1430973—dc22   2008030747

Series design by Erik Lindstrom
Cover design by Ben Peterson

Printed in the United States of America

Bang FOF 10 9 8 7 6 5 4 3 2 1

This book is printed on acid-free paper.

All links and web addresses were checked and verified to be correct at the time of publication. Because of the dynamic nature of the web, some addresses and links may have changed since publication and may no longer be valid.

Contents

1 Introduction   1

2 The Early Mail Road West   12

3 Founding Fathers   30

4 Creating the Pony Express   45

5 A Rough Western Road   63

6 "The Lonesomest Kind of Job"   79

7 Pony Riders of Endurance   93

8 The Pony Express at Trail's End   106

   Chronology   121

   Timeline   122

   Notes   124

   Bibliography   126

   Further Reading   128

   Index   131

Introduction

It all began in two frontier cities with brass bands, enthusiastic crowds, and a view to a brighter future for the ever-expanding United States. The date was April 3, 1860, and the place was St. Joseph, Missouri, a western town that had served as one of the jumping-off places for emigrants heading to the West on the Oregon Trail. The streets of St. Joseph were decked out in holiday fashion, with U.S. flags flying from nearly every building. On the Pacific Coast, 2,000 miles (3,220 kilometers) away, an equal excitement was underway on the streets of San Francisco. The day was destined to become a mile marker in the annals of U.S. history.

"THE GREAT ENTERPRISE"
Normally, the attention of the residents of these two communities would have been focused on the other issues of the day.

In spring 1860, the people of the United States were anxious about the possibility of war. For decades, Southerners and Northerners had argued over the geographic expansion of the Southern institution of slavery. Such arguments had led to violent clashes, vicious newspaper and pamphlet debates, and a host of activities that had progressively separated the country in two. There was talk of Southern states separating from the country. There was even more talk of civil war.

Another war was on the minds of some people that same spring. Out West, a war was brewing involving the Paiute (an American Indian nation) and white settlers in Nevada. Both conflicts—the potential civil war and the war in the West— could have a serious impact on the Pony Express. The Paiute lived on lands that were soon to be crossed by riders scheduled to begin delivering the mail across the country.

On this particular spring day, however, everyone was ready to play witness to an event that had been touted in the newspapers as "The Greatest Enterprise of Modern Times."[1] Some had become accustomed to such exaggerated claims, since the previous decades had seen great improvements in transportation and communication. Technology had turned the United States into a nation where innovation was at every hand and improvement and progress were the order of the day. Over the previous two generations, the country's amateur scientists, tinkerers, and mechanics had invented boats and ships powered by steam; great canals that helped link the various parts of the country; and an electromagnetic telegraph that provided instant communication, an innovation new to not just the United States, but to the entire world. Now, an enterprising businessman named William H. Russell was promising to provide mail delivery across remote regions of the country in a fraction of the time then required.

That spring, getting the U.S. mail across the great expanse of the continent was a nightmarish, complicated, and time-consuming process. Mail service from the eastern United States to California was delivered down various rivers, including the Ohio and the Mississippi, to St. Louis, Missouri, or Memphis, Tennessee. From there, it was carried by stagecoach along twisting, back-country roads to Fort Smith, Arkansas, and then along even more primitive roads to El Paso, Texas, and across the desert territories of the Southwest to Southern California. Generally, the only other alternative was to carry the mail from New York Harbor by ship to the Central American country of Panama, where it was transferred to train cars and sent by rail across the jungle landscape to the Pacific side of the isthmus. Once there, it was loaded onto a second ocean-going vessel that finally delivered the mail to San Francisco. Either way, mail delivery from one coast to the other took a minimum of three weeks. Russell's new system was promising the same in just 10 days—less than half the time.

Unlike the other recent innovations of the time, Russell's new mail delivery system was anything but high tech. It had nothing to do with steam power, except for the trains that would carry the mail from the East to St. Joseph. There were no machines, no timesaving devices, no whiz-bang electromagnetics. Russell's new system was based on one of the oldest forms of transportation known to humankind: the horse. On that day, a horse and rider in St. Joseph and a horse and rider in San Francisco were scheduled to leave their respective towns and head toward one another as fast as they could.

Over the thousands of miles between them, they would follow the same trail, one punctuated with a new string of stations where they would be relieved by fresh riders and fresh horses, each making as much progress along the trail as their endurance could manage. At each station, a rider was to take no more than two minutes to reach the facility, dismount, remove the mail pouches from his horse and transfer them to a fresh horse, remount, and get back on the trail. Each rider was to drive his horse at a relentless gallop for 35 to 75 miles (56 to 120 km), depending on the distance between stations. They were to ride night and day, without any stops. Somewhere along the trail, out in the great openness of the West, two riders would pass one another. Russell intended to deliver the mail across the continent using this vast, transcontinental relay system.

AN ANXIOUS CROWD

April 3 was the date he intended to make his promise a reality, but things started off more slowly than expected. The train scheduled to arrive from the East at 5 P.M. in St. Joseph was running late. To entertain the anxious crowd assembled there, a handler brought a horse out of the Pike's Peak Stables, "a fine bay mare."[2] The crowd watched as the stable hand led the horse around, which would help warm her up for her scheduled run. Some in the crowd took the liberty of pulling some hairs from the horse's tail as souvenirs of the day. So many hairs were removed, in fact, that a St. Joseph newspaper, *The Weekly West*, would later report how "the little pony was almost robbed of his tail."[3]

While the anxious crowd was excited somewhat by the appearance of the horse that would soon make history, they were also interested in the unique saddle kit—a saddle cover and leather pouches—that lay across the animal's back. It had been specially designed just for the new Pony Express. The saddle kit had been fashioned by a local saddle maker, Israel Landis. It was lighter and smaller, weighing only 13 pounds (5.9 kilograms), about one-third the normal weight, and lay over the horse's saddle. It was called a *mochila*, the Spanish word for "knapsack." A Pony Express rider named W.A. Cates is believed to have designed it. The pouch frame was a leather rectangle that featured four pockets, called *cantinas*, one at each corner. There were two cutouts in the mochila that were intended to accommodate a saddle's pommel and cantle. The design's purpose was to contain a rider's mail delivery in the four leather pouches and to transfer from horse to horse with ease. Speed, after all, was the key to the Pony Express's design and purpose.

The mochila could easily be pulled hurriedly from the saddle of one horse and thrown onto the back of a fresh replacement horse, allowing the rider to transfer horses at a Pony Express station within the allotted time of two minutes.

As interesting as the unique saddle covering was, it did not hold the interest of the gathered crowd for long. Local officials and dignitaries soon stepped up to speak. The first to take the stage was St. Joseph Mayor Meriwether Jeff Thompson, a local official popular with many of the community's voters. He had a warm personality, mingled easily with local townspeople, and could be so engaging that the famous writer Mark Twain would one day base a character in his novel *The Gilded Age* on Thompson. To many of his constituents, Thompson looked the part of a dignified politician, "with his impeccable taste in clothes, usually a tall gray beaver hat, tight trousers, a blue frock coat with polished brass buttons, and, around his waist, a pair of ivory-handled pistols."[4] For this occasion, he also wore a curved military saber at his side. Perhaps the only disadvantage to Thompson's appearance was that as a young man he had lost all the teeth on one side of his mouth, leaving his facial features slightly deformed. Still, his oratorical skills could spellbind his audience and move a crowd to shout their support.

As he spoke, he described the Pony Express with visionary excitement. This new mail delivery system would be the first link between East and West. It would signal the way for the building of a new railroad across the West, all the way to California. The Pony Express would not only deliver the mail; it would deliver the country's future:

> I say that the wilderness which lies between us and that El Dorado will soon blossom as the rose. Cities will spring into existence where the Indians and buffalo now hold possession. The dry and useless desert will be made to yield abundant crops. Mountains will be tunneled, streams bridged, and the iron monster which has become Mankind's slave will

Many of the romantic stories told of the Old West include the famous Pony Express, an early mail delivery system that used horses and men instead of cars and gas. When the Pony Express first began, riders did not need much in terms of equipment but had a leather pouch to hold correspondence. Called a mochila (*above*), this bag was specially designed for mail and could be quickly moved to another horse at relay stations.

ply between our confines and those far distant shores. As the Indian vanishes, the white man takes his place. Commercial activity will replace the tepee and the campfire. Schools and colleges will span the continent.[5]

Thompson's words would one day prove him to be a prophetic politician. It is no wonder he connected the Pony Express with the coming of the railroad. During the 1850s, Thompson had helped finance the construction of the Hannibal & St. Joseph Railroad, the first rail line to cross Missouri.

That railroad had played an important role in making St. Joseph the Pony Express's first station on the line's eastern end. Although San Francisco had been chosen as the western terminus for obvious reasons (it was the largest U.S. city on the Pacific Coast), Russell had selected St. Joseph over other possible western towns, including Leavenworth, Kansas. It had been selected for several important reasons: First, at that time, the town was about as far west as the East's railroads had ventured. Russell knew mail trains must support his Pony Express. In addition, the town itself had courted Russell's company by ceding large amounts of local land to the company in exchange for the benefits and honor of being selected as the Pony Express's eastern home.

Russell was the senior partner in a three-man company bearing the names of all three investors: Russell, Majors & Waddell. They had already made profits in the West providing express wagon service to miners and remote U.S. Army posts. Russell was well known to the people of St. Joseph and "locally popular in spite of his cosmopolitan dress and manner."[6] Following Mayor Thompson's energizing speech, Russell rose to the podium. Not known for his speaking, Russell kept his turn at the lectern to a minimum. Then, his partner Alexander Majors took his turn. Just as Mayor Thompson had emphasized the future of the railroad crossing the West, Majors spoke of a transcontinental rail line as evidence "of civilization and man's irresistible mania of progression."[7]

READY TO RIDE

Although such speeches brought enthusiastic cheers of support, the gathered crowd had not come to hear speeches alone. They had come to see action—to see an eager and experienced rider mount his specially equipped steed and ride off down the trail of destiny.

The train from the East bringing the mail from St. Louis had still not yet arrived. Since the first horse scheduled to leave St. Joseph had made an appearance, officials then brought out the man who would ride that horse. For many years following this first day of the Pony Express, controversy surrounded the identity of just who this historic rider was. St. Joseph's *Weekly West* reported him as "Mr. Billy Richardson, formerly a sailor, and a man accustomed to every description of hardship, having sailed for years among the snows of the Northern ocean."[8] But many in attendance that day remembered him as a young Kansas ranch hand and horse racer named Johnny Fry (possibly spelled Frye). The later loss of Pony Express records did not help clear up the matter.

It would eventually be Richardson himself who cleared things up more than 70 years later in his memoirs, by denying he had been the first rider for the St. Joseph end of the Pony Express. Richardson, the brother of the livery stable operator, had only ridden the first westward-bound Pony Express horse down to the local wharf where a steamboat carried the first rider and his mount across the Missouri River to Kansas. Indeed, the intrepid first rider had been young Fry. He was a fitting choice for St. Joseph's end of the line, having been born and raised in the frontier town. He would not be the first rider for the entire Pony Express enterprise, though. That honor would later go to James Randall, the rider out in San Francisco. He hit the trail toward the East three hours ahead of Fry, due to the delay of the arrival of the mail train back in Missouri.

Finally, after two hours of delays, the overdue train steamed into the St. Joseph train depot, a blast from its whistle informing the waiting crowd of its arrival. The story of its delay had begun days earlier. To help advertise the Pony Express, eastern railroads had sent special telegraph messages across the eastern half of the United States, and even Canada, informing rail officials where to send Pony Express mail to be picked up for the line's opening. The plan had been to have the mail carried to Hannibal, Missouri, where the Hannibal & St. Joseph Railroad would deliver it to St. Joseph. On March 30, the appointed mail courier had picked up mail in Washington, D.C., which he carried by train to New York City. He received more mail there the following day and caught a train bound for points farther west. It was in Detroit that he failed to keep to the original plan. He had missed the next train by two hours.

A telegram was sent to the superintendent of the Hannibal & St. Joseph Railroad, informing him of the mail courier's dilemma. Railroad Superintendent J.T.K. Haywood then sent out orders to have the railroad's entire line cleared, and he dispatched the courier on a special train that included the locomotive and a single passenger car. The railroad's road master, George H. Davis, prepared the train and even chose to ride along. The locomotive's engineer was Addison "Ad" Clark, known for his speed. When the courier reached Hannibal, running two and a half hours behind schedule, Davis gave instructions to "Clark to pull the throttle all the way back, to set a record that would last 50 years."[9] As the special train steamed westward across Missouri, it became the first train to run in the United States for the sole reason of delivering the mail. By 7 P.M., Clark's locomotive, the *Missouri*, reached the station at St. Joseph, where "Engineer Clark stepped majestically from his iron horse, looking mussed up, grimy, and grand . . . the hero of the hour."[10] He had covered the 206 miles

When the mail courier from Washington, D.C., finally arrived in St. Joseph, Missouri, the nation's correspondence was immediately whisked away to the awaiting Pony Express rider at Pikes Peak Stables (*above*). As part of an entire network of mail deliverymen, riders of the Pony Express had to canter through the rugged, dangerous terrain of the Western frontier to deliver messages for their customers.

(332 km) from Hannibal to St. Joseph, including a stop for water and wood, in less than five hours.

Speed continued to be the watchword even as the train arrived in St. Joseph. By 7:14, the newly arrived mail had been placed in three of the four mochila pockets and placed on the back of the first horse. (The fourth pouch was left empty for additional mail that might be picked up along the way.) By 7:15, a brass cannon was fired, and a cheer went up from the tired crowd as the rider took off down the streets of St. Joseph.

Once he had been delivered to the Kansas bank of the river, Fry headed off into the night toward Cottonwood Springs

Station, the first relay station outside St. Joseph. He arrived there an hour later, where he began the routine that would be repeated thousands of times during the Pony Express's operation. He leapt down from his horse, threw the special mochila from his tired mount over the saddle of his fresh one, remounted, and took off across the desolate Kansas prairie.

What lay ahead for this first young man to leave St. Joseph as a Pony Express rider? Would the horse line prove as effective and efficient as Russell had promised? Would the Pony Express represent a new era in mail delivery in the United States? What remote obstacles lay out there in the dark, waiting for young Fry and all his associates who would become a part of a horse and human chain across the West?

The Early Mail
Road West

Throughout the first half of the nineteenth century, the attention of the United States looked ever westward. Since the establishment of European colonies along the Atlantic coast of North America during the seventeenth century, the natural tendency of the colonists and, later, the citizens of the United States, was to move farther and farther west. The reach of the new republic extended to the Mississippi River, that great interior highway that served as the eastern border of Spanish-held Louisiana. After the United States purchased Louisiana directly from the French, the territory of the United States extended as far as the Rocky Mountains.

AN EXPANDING COUNTRY

Within two generations, other geographical plums fell into the country's lap. U.S. immigrants to the northern Mexican province of Tejas (today's Texas) led a successful revolution to overthrow the Mexican government's hold on the region during the 1830s. Texas became a U.S. state by 1845. The Oregon Country (the modern-day states of Oregon, Washington, and Idaho) was also annexed by the U.S. government by the mid-1840s.

This left only the vast Mexican provinces of the Southwest out of U.S. control. By 1846, Mexico and the United States were at war, a conflict begun through a dispute over the western border of Texas. President James K. Polk—who dreamed of annexing Mexico's remaining northern provinces extending from New Mexico to California—used the disagreement to his country's advantage. In less than two years of fighting, the U.S. Army defeated Mexico, the border of Texas was set at the Rio Grande, and Mexico's northern lands became U.S. territory.

With the transfer of northern provincial Mexican territory to the United States, high priority was now placed on establishing mail delivery between the East Coast and the newly acquired portion of the West Coast. But mail delivery had never been a sure thing, other than that it took weeks to reach the Pacific from the Atlantic. Mail might be delivered by steamship, the most reliable ocean-going vessel afloat. (Wooden clipper ships with their acres of great canvas sails might sail faster, but they were at the whim of the winds.) Still, the steamships chosen for the job had to sail a long, circuitous route of 13,000 miles (21,000 km)—equal to more than halfway around Earth's equator—around the entire continent of South America or across the Isthmus of Panama. The South American trip took six months, and crossing the isthmus might lop off only a month's travel time. Still, for all its drawbacks, mail service by ship from east to west was the best method available.

By comparison, mail delivery in the United States east of the Mississippi River was organized, relatively efficient, and speedy. Roads and waterways from town to town were common, and the delivery of everything from heavy equipment to the mail was easy enough. In addition, nearly a hundred railroad lines crisscrossed the East, each one extending from 5 to nearly 200 miles long (about 8 to 320 km), further connecting eastern communities. Along the Mississippi River alone, nearly 750 steamboats ran up and downstream. Other steamboats plied the waters of other eastern rivers. Where towns were not close enough to a river or major thoroughfare, canals had been constructed. Stagecoach lines provided additional connections, often rambling their way along poorly built roads, but reaching their destinations on schedule. In the East, the national postal service, which operated 18,000 post offices east of the Mississippi River, used all these systems—stagecoaches, steamboats, canal packets, and railroads—to deliver the mail.

Mail, of course, did not just mean letters or personal correspondence any more than it does today. The mail included newspapers, government papers, and privately printed materials of all sorts, including business documents. The U.S. mail also included, especially over long distances, such things as currency and bank notes. For everyone, the faster and more efficiently these postmarked papers could find their way to each recipient, the better.

The creation of mail delivery systems did not happen overnight. Since the establishment of the United States during the Revolutionary War of the 1770s and 1780s, the government had taken on the task and obligation of seeing that the nation's mail was delivered. That task typically did not include the actual *delivery* of the mail. Usually, the government contracted with private companies and individuals as mail carriers. Such privately contracted carriers might use any and all existing transportation systems, or even create a few of their own.

In all of this private contracting, the government still played other vital roles. It was up to the members of the U.S. Congress to establish new postal routes. Congress would then make such decisions as how often the mail should be delivered between two locales, and how much the government was willing to pay to those contracted to provide actual mail service. Once those criteria were established, the nation's postmaster general would advertise the new postal route and begin taking private bids for the new mail route's contract. Once a mail contractor was chosen, a contract was drawn up. If the individual or company contracted did not live up to the government's expectations, the contract could be cancelled. If a contractor who received a contract eventually realized he had bid too low and could not deliver the mail as expected and still make a profit, he could appeal to Congress to raise his compensation. Congressmen were usually not open to renegotiating agreements. Such contractors had signed an agreement understanding they were taking on risks, but the lure of profits caused many to gamble that they could deliver the nation's mail efficiently and effectively.

STEAMSHIPS TO DELIVER THE MAIL

To alleviate the problem of mail delivery to the West, Congress passed a bill in March 1847 approving the construction of five steamships to be used for mail delivery to the Pacific coast. The program was placed under the leadership of the U.S. secretary of the Navy, but the government had no intention of taking a hands-on role in mail delivery across the continent. The Navy secretary was authorized to grant 10-year contracts with two separate companies to provide transcontinental mail service. One company was to transport the mail from the Atlantic coast and New Orleans to California where the second company was to provide mail service to other West Coast destinations. Entrepreneur Arnold Harris received the contract to deliver the mail to and from East to West, and the second contract went to a businessman named A.G. Sloo. The following year, Sloo sold out to another investor, William H. Aspinwall, who established the Pacific Mail Steamship Company in the spring of 1848.

That autumn, mail delivery began involving the first of the government's five mail steamships, the *California*, which steamed out of New York Harbor in early October. The ship was bound for the Pacific Coast via the long way around South America. The government's plan for reliable mail delivery was underway and on schedule. But other events would soon interfere with West Coast mail delivery. When the ship sailed from its docks, news of the discovery of gold in Northern California had not yet reached the ports in the East. Docking in Callao, Peru, after nearly three months at sea, the ship's crew was stunned by both the news and the hundreds of locals who wanted to take passage on the *California* to reach the quickly expanding gold camps outside Sacramento. Although built to house no more than 100 passengers, the mail delivery vessel took on more than 400 eager gold seekers. When the *California* reached San Francisco, not only did the would-be prospectors disembark, but the ship's entire crew did, too. The U.S. mail from the East Coast remained onboard.

In time, however, mail delivery by steamship became a matter of routine, and such vessels were soon carrying large amounts of mail. The people of San Francisco came to rely heavily on this government-sponsored service. So anticipated was each ship's arrival and delivery of news from the East Coast and beyond, that on days when such steamers were due to arrive, spotters would mount local Telegraph Hill to keep a sharp eye out. Once a ship was spotted, semaphores (special flags used to indicate letters and numbers) were used to signal the arrival to the public. It seemed that so many in San Francisco were so anxious for the arrival of the mail steamers that they learned the coded flag signals themselves.

Mail delivery by steamship still took months, though, and it was an expensive system to support. Each year, the service provided by the government-authorized steamships cost about $700,000 even as postage revenue to the government ran closer to $200,000. With the system hemorrhaging $500,000 annually, the steamships were arriving with regularity, but at a severe loss. In addition, because the trip around South America took

Before the development of overland mail delivery, coast-to-coast corre-spondence traveled by steamship. This method proved to be inefficient and expensive, especially as more people migrated west to become miners or settlers. Frustrated, citizens were soon urging Congress for government subsidies to help fund a mail system that would travel by land rather than by sea. Above, the U.S. mail steamship *Clara* sailing near Florida.

so long, once news arrived on the West or East coasts, it could hardly be called news. When a railroad was built across the Isthmus of Panama by early 1855, the time of delivery was cut, but the system was still costly and slow.

In time, some began to consider the possibilities of deliver-ing the mail across the United States by land, rather than by ship. The distance was certainly shorter, but land travel was just about as slow. There were no rail tracks running west of the Mississippi River. The only lengthy, navigable river for steamboat travel was the Missouri, but "although steamboats plied this waterway, its wandering northwesterly course led nowhere near the Pacific Coast."[1] What few stagecoaches there were in the West were short runs. As for roads, they were little more than places where enough traffic had worn down the grasses to make them obvious.

AN OVERLAND MAIL ROUTE

Nevertheless, the government did agree to an arrangement to deliver the mail overland. To connect mail delivery from Salt Lake City back East, the government entered into an agreement with Samuel H. Woodson, who ran a stagecoach service between the Mormon settlement and Independence, Missouri. Independence was one of the most important jumping-off places for pioneers heading to the West along the Oregon Trail. Woodson received $19,500 to deliver the mail between those two western towns for four years.

Although nearly $20,000 was a tidy sum in the 1850s (historians suggest that such figures may be multiplied by 100 to approximate the amount in modern dollars), Woodson had agreed to a considerable undertaking. He intended to deliver mail over a section of the Oregon Trail 1,200 miles (1,930 km) long, across rugged terrain, a third of which included mountains. The agreement also stipulated that Woodson establish a system that delivered the mail from Missouri to Utah every 30 days, relying on little more than pack animals and wagons. Wagon trains of mountain men and pioneer immigrants had been traveling the Oregon Trail for two decades, and such trains typically took nearly three months to cover the same ground.

Woodson had agreed to a near impossibility and still expected to make a profit. Without establishing relief stations of his own, the trail between both ends of his mail route only provided three stops where his draught animals, tired from the trail, could be replaced. These stops were Fort Kearny in Nebraska, and Fort Laramie and Fort Bridger in Wyoming. In addition, mail deliveries over the trail during the winter months would be impractical, if not deadly. By 1851, Woodson was in a panic, fearing he would lose his mail contract. He then made his own agreement with a resident of Salt Lake City, Feramorz Little, who took over the leg of the mail route between Fort Laramie and Salt Lake City, with both men agreeing to hand off mail to one another on the fifteenth of each month at Laramie.

Such coordination proved impossible, as weather problems could not be negotiated away. During one November delivery, Little and his teamsters were caught in a blizzard in Wyoming's South Pass and nearly died. They were forced to abandon their animals, throw away the printed materials in the mail, and only deliver the letters to Salt Lake City. They ended their run by carrying the remaining mail 40 miles (64 km) on foot through heavy snows.

Through the four-year run of Woodson's contract, the mail service was generally adequate, certainly better than it had been in previous years. Still, it was often late and sometimes damaged by rain and snow. When Mormon leader Brigham Young wrote a letter to one of his territorial congressmen, he included a criticism of the region's mail delivery system: "So little confidence have we in the present mail arrangement that we feel considerable [doubt] of your receiving this or any other communication from us."[2] Woodson gave up his contract after these four discouraging years.

By contracting with Woodson to only deliver the mail to Salt Lake City, the government still had to work out an agreement for postal service between the Mormon capital and Sacramento, California, a distance of almost 1,000 miles (1,600 km). The contract went to two men destined to experience many of the same miseries as Woodson and Little—Absalom

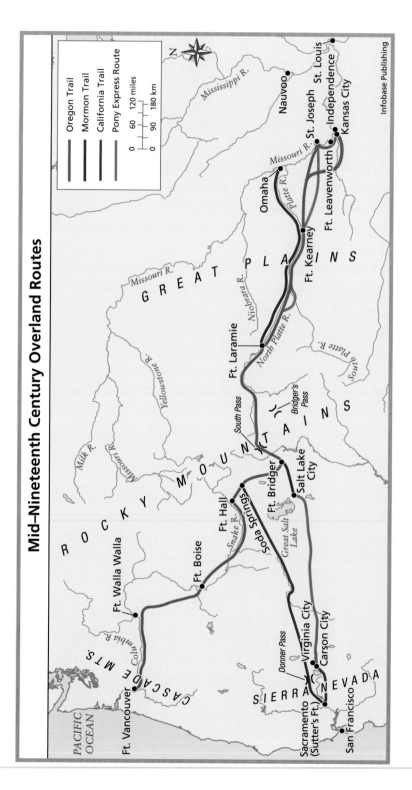

Mid-Nineteenth Century Overland Routes

Oregon Trail
Mormon Trail
California Trail
Pony Express Route

0   60   120 miles
0   90   180 km

Infobase Publishing

Woodward and George Chorpenning. They, too, agreed to monthly mail delivery, relying on pack mules, and were to be paid $14,000 by the government. They also learned from Woodson and divided the distance into two halves, with each operating his own leg of the route.

As with Woodson's route, things did not go well. Chorpenning opened the route when he left Sacramento on May 1, 1851, on horseback, carrying 75 pounds (34 kg) of mail. He only managed to reach Salt Lake City after 53 difficult days through the mountains and across the Nevada desert. He had encountered heavy snows in the Sierra Nevada Mountains, which only helped to prove to some critics that a central mail route across the West was impractical and that a better route would cross the southern regions of modern-day Arizona and New Mexico.

Absalom Woodward met an untimely death six months after opening the mail route that spring. During the November delivery, Woodward and his employees—four veteran mountain men, each armed with the latest government-issued, long-range rifles—were attacked by 70 American Indians at Clover Patch, along the Humboldt River in Utah Territory. The mail party fought off the attackers after killing several of them. They continued on their way, covering as much ground as possible by not stopping that night. The following day, they encountered Chorpenning and his men and warned the westbound

(*opposite*) **Like the pioneers who were traveling west on the Oregon Trail, Pony Express riders had to endure trips over mountains and through a desert. Survival, however, would not be the riders' only challenge, as they also had to reach their destination in a timely manner. While groups of settlers would normally take 6 months to complete the Oregon Trail, Samuel H. Woodson hoped his new delivery service could travel along part of the same route over 30 days.**

party to be on the lookout. Woodward could not know that his party was still in danger: American Indians were following his group, seeking blood vengeance for their lost warriors.

When Chorpenning's group passed the American Indians, they were simply ignored from a distance. Woodward and his men, however, were attacked a second time along the Humboldt River, where all four of the mountain men were killed and Woodward wounded. Jumping on his horse, Woodward managed to ride 150 miles (240 km) away before falling from his saddle and dying alone in the desert.

Chorpenning continued to struggle along without his business partner, but stories of the massacre spread like wildfire, making hiring a new mail delivery crew difficult. By 1852, Chorpenning was making some of his mail deliveries unescorted. Because of his dedicated service, he was granted a second mail contract in 1854, and got his first break in delivering mail. The government changed the route from Sacramento to San Diego, hundreds of miles further south. From there, the mail was delivered north to San Francisco by ship. This new delivery trail allowed Chorpenning to avoid the snows of the Sierra Nevada, making winter delivery more reliable.

In another four years, he was granted yet another mail contract, this time to deliver mail from Salt Lake City to Placerville, California, in the heart of the gold camp country. This new route was a stagecoach line, making mail delivery much easier than it was by pack mule, as well as faster. The route was named Egan's Trail, after Howard Egan, who established it. The trail followed the Humboldt River south and included stage stops spaced every 20 miles or so (30 km) at locations that included Rush Valley, Deep Creek, Ruby Valley, Smith's Creek, and Buckland's Station.

This new line did not pan out for Chorpenning. The mail entrepreneur spent $300,000 establishing the new mail route, but the government's subsidy only amounted to $180,000, which was later reduced to $160,000, and then cut in half. With such a financial drain, Chorpenning surrendered his contract with the government in 1860. In the meantime, the government had worked out a new southern route for mail delivery that was also based on a stagecoach line.

THE BUTTERFIELD LINE

In the fall of 1858, the new line was established through a six-year contract with the Butterfield Overland Mail Company, which was formed through the collaboration of four Western express firms: Adams, American, National, and Wells, Fargo & Company. The line had come about after 1856 when California Senator John B. Weller presented a pair of volumes, "bound in hand-tooled leather,"[3] to the presiding officer of the Senate. The books contained a petition signed by 75,000 Californians eager for the government to finance the opening of a new road across the Southwest to accommodate a new, reliable, transcontinental stagecoach line.

By August 1856, Congress authorized a mail contract for a stage line that would follow a route that, according to one critic, went "from no place through nothing to nowhere."[4] The slated line was to run from San Antonio, Texas, to San Diego. The line would connect with a route between New Orleans and the home of the Alamo, and would cover nearly 1,500 miles of remote desert country.

This first stage line proved a dismal failure. Its original contractor, 29-year-old James Birch, died on board the steamship *Central America* when the vessel capsized during a violent storm off the Florida coast. The contract was handed off to another businessman, George Giddings, whose line between San Antonio and San Diego became a miserable failure. Coaches sometimes could not complete the journey across the desert, and pack mules instead delivered the mail. (Since the early stages on this line relied on mules rather than horses, it was popularly referred to as the "Jackass Line.") The line proved unpopular and a financial disaster. During its four years of operation, fewer than a hundred people took passage on the line's stages, and mail revenue was miniscule, supported by government subsidy. Costs ran so high that "every letter delivered between San Antonio and San Diego cost the government approximately $65."[5]

The government was forced to admit the line's failure, but the need for a serviceable stage line, one that could reliably deliver the mail, was still there. On September 15, 1857, after the "Jackass Line" had only been in business for a year, Congress authorized the establishment of another line across the Southwest. It appropriated $600,000 annually to provide semiweekly mail delivery by stagecoach between "such point on the Mississippi River as the contractors may select, to San Francisco."[6] The postmaster general, a Southerner named Aaron Brown, selected two terminals in the East for the line, at St. Louis and Memphis, Tennessee, his hometown.

The line was designated to first run along two roads to Fort Smith, Arkansas, where the dual routes would meld into one. From Fort Smith, the line would run in a great, dipping arc south into Texas to El Paso, then across the Southwest to Fort Yuma near Mexico's border, and bend northward to Los Angeles and San Francisco along the California coast. In all, the new route would cover a distance across the West of nearly 2,800 miles. Because of its arc, the line was referred to as "the oxbow route" and "the horseshoe." Some Northerners regretted the loss of revenue a northern line would have provided and also feared that the extremely southern route would encourage the expansion of slavery into the Southwest. The line appeared to some to stretch unnecessarily long, perhaps as much as 1,000 miles more than needed. The *Chicago Tribune* labeled the legislation creating the new line as "one of the greatest swindles ever perpetrated upon the country by the slaveholders."[7] Even Californians were critical of the proposed route, concerned it would only lengthen the time for mail delivery. The *Sacramento Union* newspaper called the line "a Panama route by land."[8]

The new company would become a titanic operation, involving 800 employees, 250 Abbott and Downing stagecoaches, the legendary Concord stage, and corrals filled with 1,800 horses and mules. The company would construct 139 relay stations, establish a relative road, and build bridges across streams. All this was necessary to provide stagecoach service across the desolate reaches of the West.

The man responsible for it all was the one appointed by Postmaster General Brown—John Butterfield. Almost anyone in the United States might have considered the work required to establish a new, elongated stagecoach line across the country as a task too daunting for words. New Yorker Butterfield, however, took to the project with enthusiasm and a keen business eye. Butterfield was familiar with the operation of stagecoaches, having worked as a stage driver as a young man. By the middle of the century, he held controlling interest in most of the important stagecoach lines in New York State. He also had helped establish the American Express Company, which was destined to become one of the largest corporations in the country. (Today's American Express is descended from this original company.)

Armed with his $600,000 annual government subsidy, Butterfield added funds from his other corporate interests to the tune of $1 million, and established the new stage line with an eye to every detail. Although his contract called for mail delivery by stage on a one-way schedule of 25 days, Butterfield planned for his stages to cover the entire distance of the line in 24 days or fewer, figuring on his stagecoaches covering 4.5 miles per hour. By purchasing Concord stagecoaches, Butterfield was ensuring the best quality stage that money could buy, even if they were not comfortable by any modern standards. Though passenger service would always be an important part of the Butterfield Line's design and purpose, the businessman always reminded his employees of their main task: "Remember, boys, nothing on God's earth must stop the U.S. Mail."[9]

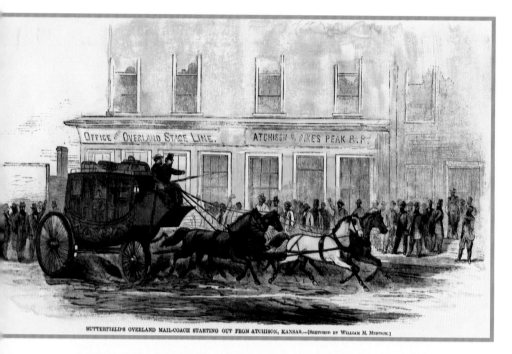

BUTTERFIELD'S OVERLAND MAIL-COACH STARTING OUT FROM ATCHISON, KANSAS.—[SKETCHED BY WILLIAM M. MERRICK.]

Businessman John Butterfield signed a contract with the federal government to begin an experimental mail delivery service from Missouri and Tennessee to the West Coast. Using mainly stagecoaches for transportation, about 500-600 packages and letters were carried almost 2,800 miles across the country on a semiweekly basis.

By September 15, 1858, a year to the day after Congress authorized the establishment of the nation's longest stagecoach line, the first stagecoaches of the Butterfield Line were ready to roll. Passengers paid $200 for a ticket to take the stage from the Mississippi River to California. Butterfield had planned his new route so closely that even on its maiden trip, the first westbound stage completed its trek in 24 days, 18 hours, and 26 minutes, arriving on October 10. The first eastbound stage reached St. Louis the previous day, 44 hours ahead of schedule. Through coordination and planning, the Butterfield Line ran stages twice a week, remaining generally on schedule. Some stages even finished the trip in as few as 21 days. For passengers,

WILLIAM BAYARD

Asking for More Than
Congress Could Deliver

From the inception of the United States as a new country in the late eighteenth century and well into the nineteenth century, Congress regularly entered into contracts with private individuals to deliver the nation's mail, especially over long distances. Sometimes, would-be mail contractors were motivated by little more than dollar signs. During the late 1840s, one such entrepreneur was William Bayard, a businessman who proposed an elaborate system for delivering the U.S. mail overland from Arkansas to California—all for a handsome profit.

Bayard's overwrought plan was to provide transcontinental mail delivery along a southerly route between Fort Smith, Arkansas, and San Diego, California. He intended to establish this stagecoach route across the Southwest to deliver not only the U.S. mail, but also freight and passengers. One problem, however, was that no stagecoach road, or even any viable road of any type, existed between Arkansas and California. Undeterred, Bayard agreed to establish the stage line and build the road needed. To provide materials for his road, Bayard asked the government to grant him permission to use the timber and stone on all government property the road would cross. He did agree that after 15 years of service, the road and all improvements, including any bridges, would be returned to the ownership of the U.S. government.

Since such a road would pass through American Indian country, including Apache lands, Bayard proposed to erect stagecoach stations every 10 or 15 miles (16 to 24 km) along the trail. Each station would employ 50 armed guards to provide security for stage passengers and to guarantee the delivery of the mail. In exchange

(continues)

(continued)

for this road construction and the establishment and operation of a stagecoach line across the Southwest, Bayard requested the right to charge tolls to anyone else who might use the road. The toll money would be used to provide upkeep along the route. He also wanted the right to purchase 4 square miles (about 10 square kilometers) of land along every 30 miles (48 km) of his planned route. His requested purchase price was 10 cents an acre, much lower than the going rate for government land. To top off his request to Congress, Bayard wanted to receive an annual government stipend of $750,000.

Unfortunately for Bayard, his dreams of his proposed stagecoach line and easy profits never became a reality. Congressmen believed he was overreaching in his expectations, and he was turned down. Those who received later contracts to deliver the mail across the West based their promises on more modest proposals.

however, it was not a pleasant trip. One rider described the route as "the worst road God ever built."[10] Over the roughest parts of the route, the fancier Concord stages were not used, with the line relying instead on "celerity wagons," vehicles stripped of excess weight and comfort and designed for wear and tear.

All Butterfield's planning paid off. Although some Californians had been critical of the elongated route at first, the vast majority came to appreciate the regular arrival of Butterfield stagecoaches to their communities. Each arrival was heralded with a blast of the stage horn carried by the coach's driver. As one passenger of the line wrote in the *New York Post*:

> The blast of the stage horn as it rolls through the valleys and over the prairies of the West cheers and gladdens the heart of the pioneer. As it sounds through the valleys of Santa Clara and San Jose, it sends a thrill of delight to the Californian. He knows that it brings tidings from the hearts and homes he left behind him; it binds him stronger and firmer to his beloved country."[11]

The line suffered from its share of problems, of course. The route crossed American Indian country where hostile Apache, Comanche, and Kiowa considered the stagecoaches to be an intrusion. Despite its problems, however, the Butterfield Line was considered a success, and its end came too abruptly with the outbreak of the Civil War in 1861. With the opening of the war, Confederate raiders also considered the federally sponsored stagecoach line to be an intrusion, and soon bridges and stations along the line were destroyed. Even so, throughout the short run of the Butterfield Stagecoach Line, the long, arcing road across the Southwest delivered more mail than all the ships at sea.

Founding
Fathers

The Butterfield line was one of the first casualties to fall with the outbreak of the Civil War in spring 1861. The route fell under control of Confederate forces, who destroyed the line so it could not be used by stagecoaches subsidized by their enemy, the federal government. Once again, a northern or central route received renewed support as the most viable option for transcontinental mail delivery. But, as earlier entrepreneurs knew, a mail service route that followed the Oregon Trail and entered California through the Sierra Nevada was difficult and dangerous. Woodson, Woodward, and Chorpenning had discovered these realities the hard way, losing either their fortunes or their very lives.

Nevertheless, a central route remained the only option for Northerners wanting to stay connected to the Pacific coast. (Oregon and California, after all, remained loyal to the Union during the war.) With earlier wagon and pack animal mail routes having been unbearably slow, those considering a new line were eager to try other means. Talk soon circulated, suggesting that the key might lie in a single horse and rider carrying the mail. They would have greater speed and would be more likely to achieve success over difficult terrain or through intimidating winter weather than a system based on wagons or stagecoaches.

AN OLD SYSTEM REVISITED

The idea of a delivery system based on a relay of mail from one horseback rider to another was not new in the 1860s. The ancient Persian Empire relied on such a system to keep all corners of its vast Near East kingdom connected and informed. The very word *postal* originally referred to the system of wooden poles or posts that were erected along Persian roads where letters and other mail could be tacked to be picked up by mail carriers.

A similar pony and rider relay system was established by the Mongol conqueror of China, Genghis Khan. The Venetian trader Marco Polo described the great Khan's system. Stations were built about 25 miles (40 km) apart, allowing a single rider to cover as many as 300 miles (480 km) in a single day by switching regularly to fresh horses. During the 1820s, such a scaled-down system had been used in the United States between New York and Boston to deliver news faster from city to city. A system running 100 miles (160 km) from one city in the East to another along fairly established roads was one thing; to try and duplicate the same over a distance of 2,000 miles (3,200 km) of rugged territory that included hostile American Indian lands was another.

Still, the idea began to take root. It remains unclear today just who should be given credit for first considering the Pony Express that would become reality by the early 1860s. The credit might go to Henry O'Rielly who, in 1849, suggested to members of Congress that a telegraph line be strung across the West between St. Louis and California. The idea was almost immediately rejected as too outlandish. (The telegraph, invented by the American Samuel F.B. Morse, was only five years old.) In 1852, O'Rielly made another proposal for a telegraph line in the West, emphasizing that the line could be protected by establishing a string of stations along it, placed about 20 miles (32 km) apart and manned with 20 or so soldiers each. The soldiers could protect the telegraph crews who built the line. O'Rielly also thought that, since a string of stations would already be in place, the mail could be delivered between the stations, allowing for transcontinental delivery—in effect, the nation's first cross-country Pony Express. This time, Senator Stephen Douglas of Illinois agreed to present O'Rielly's plan in the spring of 1852. Despite heavy debate, the proposed bill almost passed, but then other issues of the day took up Congress's time. Thus the Pony Express proposal was defeated.

Historians also believe that the creator of the Pony Express could have been B.F. Ficklin, who served during the early 1850s as general superintendent for the giant freight and stagecoach company Russell, Majors & Waddell. In 1854, Ficklin and a California senator named William M. Gwin rode the Oregon Trail eastward from San Francisco. During their trip, Ficklin explained his idea to the senator for a horse and rider relay system to deliver the country's mail across the West, between St. Joseph and Sacramento, in an unimaginable 10 days. During the following legislative session, Senator Gwin introduced a bill in support of Ficklin's proposal. Again, shortsighted legislators defeated the bill.

Another early supporter of a horse-run mail system was Frederick A. Bee, a partner in the Placerville, Humboldt & Salt Lake City Telegraph Company. During the mid-1850s, Bee apparently spoke of such a relay line to several newspapers in San Francisco. His plan was to build a horse relay line to deliver the mail between the Missouri River and Sacramento. The line would not need to go any farther, since a telegraph line already connected the California capital with San Francisco. His idea, however, never received the financial backing he sought.

Still another important advocate for the establishment of the Pony Express was businessman William H. Russell of Russell, Majors & Waddell. It appears that in spring 1858 he discussed with U.S. Secretary of War John B. Floyd the possibility of opening a horse relay system. In winter 1859, Russell began ordering some of his employees who were based in the West to begin putting together a plan for a horse-run mail system between Sacramento and St. Joseph, Missouri. The line might be able to deliver the mail within 12 days through a relay system.

Although the list of early advocates for a horse relay system included several likely candidates, it was Russell who took the reins and began developing the idea. In early 1860, Russell met with Senator Gwin, who had supported the idea in Congress for more than five years. Gwin presented a bill to his colleagues, only to meet with opposition from Southern Congressmen who did not want to support a central mail route across the West, perhaps at the expense of Butterfield's South-based line. Others were skeptical that lone riders could cross the great expanse of the Central Plains and the Rockies, not to mention the Sierra, and deliver the mail in less than two weeks. Russell would have to prove his plan. Before he left Washington, D.C., Russell committed his company to the establishment of a transcontinental horse-run mail system.

THE PONY EXPRESS'S TRIO

Russell hurriedly left the capital and returned to his company's headquarters in Leavenworth, Kansas, to confer with his business partners, Alexander Majors and William B. Waddell. All three men had already staked a claim in the West by operating the largest freight wagon company in the country, a system that delivered supplies to western towns and river ports, Army

Despite the past failures of other courier companies, William H. Russell believed he could develop and organize an efficient, reliable service to deliver the mail across the United States. Russell's delivery plan would take approximately 12 days for mail to travel from Missouri to California, an estimate that was met with skepticism and doubt.

posts, and mining camps. For all Russell's enthusiasm about a horse relay system, though, Majors and Waddell did not like the idea. They did not believe such a system could make a profit and knew that just creating it would be an extremely expensive undertaking, government contract or no government contract. But Russell told his business associates that he had already committed the company to the plan. As one of the most respected firms in the United States, Russell, Majors & Waddell could not break such a promise. The matter was settled. The three partners then turned to pouring their energies into creating a system of stations and corrals, purchasing horses, and advertising for riders.

Who were these three entrepreneurs from the West willing to gamble on a tenuous line designed only to deliver the country's mail over thousands of miles of hostile territory? How had they come together as business partners in the first place? Their individual backgrounds provide some insight.

A FRONTIER ENTREPRENEUR

William Russell was born on January 31, 1812, the descendant of an English lord who, in 1683, was beheaded for plotting against King Charles II. William's grandfather immigrated to the United States a century later and settled in Vermont. Young William never knew his father, who died in 1814 as a commander during the War of 1812. When his mother remarried, her new husband was appointed as a government official out West for the Iowa Indian Agency. This necessitated moving his family to western Missouri. Only a teenager, William Russell was discovering life on the frontier.

He left home at the age of 16 and moved to Liberty, Missouri. The region—including St. Joseph, Independence, and Westport—would soon be famous as a starting point for the Oregon Trail. Russell worked as a clerk in several general stores before taking a position in the mercantile firm of James Gull and Samuel Ringo. In 1830, when Russell was just 18 years old, Gull and Ringo promoted him to operate their mercantile in Lexington, Missouri. He gained valuable experience there, operating a business that included bookkeeping, bill collection, and shuffling invoices, as well as the more mundane tasks of lighting the store's fire each morning and sweeping up each evening.

At age 23, Russell married Harriet Elliot Warder, whose father was a Baptist minister who had built a church on his own property, allowing him to "preach whatever he pleased."[1] Two years later, in 1837, Russell left Gull and Ringo and opened up a general store of his own, partnered with two other businessmen. An economic depression that had begun the same year Russell opened his store made success difficult, and the store failed after a few years of operation. Russell wasted little time opening another mercantile, one that proved a success. He was becoming a prosperous leading citizen of Lexington and began buying up real estate, including 3,000 acres (1,200 hectares) of local farmland. By the age of 35, Russell was wealthy, a successful businessman, and still intent on investing in new enterprises.

In 1847, he began to look to the West for new opportunity. All across the western frontier, the U.S. government was establishing distant forts and other military outposts, many of them quite remote from any town or significant settlement. Each needed to be supplied on a regular basis. Other Missourians were already involved in taking merchandise and other supplies along a great southwestern trail to the Mexican provincial town of Santa Fe, New Mexico. Russell, along with his business partner James H. Bullard and fellow investor E.C. McCarty of Westport, Missouri, organized a wagon train loaded with trade goods bound for Santa Fe. Theirs was "the first wagon train ever to carry civilian cargo from Westport Landing to Santa Fe."[2] The effort proved extremely profitable, so Russell and his partners sent another wagon train across the Southwest the following year.

In 1848, Russell, along with a new partner, James Brown, sent a similar wagon train of supplies and goods to a military post along the Santa Fe Trail, one under the command of Colonel S.W. Kearny. (Brown had already freighted for the Army the previous year, having contracted to deliver 200,000 pounds of goods to the post at Santa Fe, a success that Russell had not failed to note.) These freight operations in the West netted handsome profits for Russell and his partners. By 1850, they were overseeing the overland freighting of 600,000 pounds of supplies to U.S. military posts across the west, primarily those strung along the Santa Fe Trail. There were still many more such posts that needed what Russell was willing to provide.

Russell, in the meantime, was prospering more than ever, so much so that he purchased a 20-room mansion in Lexington, located at the corner of South and Fourteenth streets. He established other business ventures, including an insurance company. He used his money to open the Lexington Female Collegiate Institute. Russell's star continued to rise.

AN EARLY WESTERN FREIGHTER

It was in church that Russell met future freighting partner William Waddell. In the early 1850s, they partnered in a company named for themselves: Waddell & Russell. In 1854, they brought in their third partner and the freighting company became Russell, Majors & Waddell. From the beginning, Russell was always the eager risk taker, a man willing to bet on a profit. Waddell was a more conservative, quieter member of the partnership, who balanced Russell's ambition.

Waddell was of Scottish descent. His grandfather, John Waddell, immigrated to the New World during the colonial period as an apprentice to a man named Carter. Waddell's father, also named John, married Catherine Bradford, who was descended from William Bradford, the leader of Plymouth

Colony in modern-day Massachusetts. Their first child, William Bradford Waddell, was born on October 14, 1807.

By age five, William Waddell's mother died, and at age seven his father moved the family from Virginia to the western territory of Kentucky. At age 17, William set out on his own, landing a job in the lead mines near Galena, Illinois. Finding the work backbreaking and low-paying, he moved on to St. Louis, the thriving frontier river town, where he took a position as a clerk in a mercantile. The white-collar job suited him, and he soon thought of his own possibilities for future success. He returned to Kentucky for a time, where he clerked at another store and then worked at his father's farm. He later married Susan Byram, a young woman from a wealthy family. Her dowry provided enough money for Waddell to open up his own dry goods store in Mayslick, Kentucky.

The store was a success, in part due to Waddell's head for bookkeeping and business in general, but he had dreams of even greater success. He began to consider the potential of entering into the freighting business and operating, in effect, stores on wheels. By the mid 1830s, he sold his store and moved his family to Lexington, Missouri, on the edge of the frontier. Everything he touched turned to gold. He opened a new store along Lexington's waterfront and was soon able to build a large house "across the street from his new friend, William Russell."[3] Together, they had already invested in establishing several companies including the Lexington Mutual Fire & Marine Insurance Company. In 1852, he and Russell formed Waddell & Russell, and began freighting supplies to Fort Riley, Kansas, and Fort Union, New Mexico, the following year. It was a modest beginning to the freighting business for both men. In a few more years, they brought on their third partner, Alexander Majors.

A MAN OF THE TRAIL

Majors, as with his two business partners, came from simple roots. He had grown up "on the Missouri frontier in a one-window log cabin his father built."[4] His grandfather had served during the Revolutionary War under George Washington. His father, Benjamin Majors, was raised in North Carolina during the 1790s. By 1800, the Majors family moved to Kentucky to farm, where Benjamin met "a tall, beautiful Irish woman" by the name of Laurania Kelly.[5] Alexander would be their first child.

By 1820, with Missouri statehood just around the corner, Benjamin loaded his family in a covered wagon and hauled them out to the western Missouri frontier. Alexander was only six years old. The trip did not go well. One day, when the wagon careened down a hill, Benjamin Majors had to toss Alexander and his younger brother to safety. Benjamin was nearly killed. In another wagon accident, Laurania was injured and died several months later. With his mother gone, Alexander had to work hard to help his father on their new farm. Difficulties continued to stalk the Majors family over the following year, including a grasshopper infestation that destroyed their crops and those of their neighbors in less than a day. Alexander learned firsthand the harsh realities of frontier farming.

In 1827, Benjamin Majors and a couple dozen of their neighbors went West into the Rockies to search for silver. Alexander was left to care for his siblings and the farm. Gone nearly half a year, Alexander's father almost starved to death and returned home having found no silver.

Young Majors married in 1834, and he and his wife lived on a plot of land given to them by Benjamin. The couple soon had three daughters. Life was difficult, as Alexander worried how he would continue working his farmland without any sons to help him. When the Mexican-American War broke out in 1846, Alexander joined a unit of Missouri volunteers and saw action in the Mexican province of Chihuahua, where he was wounded in a fierce battle.

Returning to Missouri meant returning to the difficult life of a frontier Missouri farmer. Majors soon sought a way out of that difficult life's work. He began using his wagon to haul crops for his neighbors to market in neighboring Independence, Missouri. Seeing small profits from his new venture, he borrowed money and purchased 5 additional wagons and 78 oxen. Soon, he landed a contract to freight supplies from Independence to Santa Fe. His freighting business was expanding. He bought six wagons and loaded each with about two tons of goods. That fall, he and his employees made a record-breaking trek along the Santa Fe Trail, making the round trip in 92 days and netting a profit of $650 per wagon. He went again in 1849, this time with 20 wagons and 100 oxen, earning $13,000 in profit. His efficiency and success soon gained Majors a high reputation in the freighting business. Among those who heard of him were Waddell and Russell.

The 1850s brought Majors greater success. He won a contract in 1850 to deliver more than 50 tons of supplies to Fort Mann, near present-day Dodge City, Kansas. When he reached the fort, it was still under construction and he hired out his wagons to haul logs from a creek bottom 25 miles (40 km) from the new military outpost, making more money still. In 1851, he signed a lucrative contract with the U.S. government to supply additional frontier posts. The contract brought so much business that Majors had to add another 25 wagons and 300 oxen to his rolling stock. Two years later, he contracted to deliver supplies to Fort Union, which involved 100 wagons, 1,200 oxen, and a party of 120 employees including bullwhackers, wranglers, and freight men. The success of fulfilling this contract brought him new wealth and prestige in the freighting business and produced a new level of competition for Waddell and Russell. That same year, Waddell and Russell did not receive a single new contract from the government.

JOINING FORCES

The timing was right for the three men to join forces. Previously, the government had contracted relatively small contracts

Due to its increased Western expansion, the U.S. government decided to award only one large mail delivery contract instead of its usual practice of employing smaller companies. Alexander Majors, William H. Russell, and William Waddell combined their own individual services and talents to become the largest delivery service in the West. Their hard work and reputations soon helped them secure the federal freighting contracts. Above, a monument to the Russell, Majors, and Waddell company.

with relatively small freight operators, but the scope of army contracts was expanding as the government's military presence across the West grew. By 1854, to streamline its freighting contracts, a single, massive agreement was arranged that would run for two years to supply many of the army's outposts in the West. Only a large-scale freighter could fulfill such a contract's

(continues on page 44)

ALEXANDER MAJORS
(1814–1900)

Faith and Freighting

Western freighting magnates William Russell and William Waddell met attending the same Baptist church, but it was Alexander Majors who would be remembered as a freighter of faith. That was no small task considering the reputation of many freight men, including the teamsters and bullwhackers who drove the freight wagons. Such men were often rough and tumble, not to mention profane. On one occasion, as Majors was interviewing a potential bullwhacker, he asked the man if he was capable of driving a team of oxen hundreds of miles along a rugged trail without uttering any profanities. The man's reply was telling: "Why, I can drive to hell and back without swearing!"*

Majors held to his religious convictions and the reputation that came with it all his life. While taking wagons along a trail, he required his freight wagon caravans to uphold the Sabbath and not travel on that day. This provided a day of reflection for his employees, as well as a day of rest for his oxen. He was known for handing out leather-bound Bibles to his freight workers, who had to sign an agreement vowing their best behavior while working for Majors:

I, _____, do hereby swear, before the Great and Living God, that during my engagement, and while I am an employee of Russell, Majors & Waddell, I will, under no circumstances, use profane language; that I will drink no intoxicating liquors; that I will not quarrel or fight with any other employee of the firm, and that in every respect I will conduct myself honestly, be faithful to my duties, and so direct all my acts as to win the confidence of my employers. So help me God.**

It was a pledge that Majors soberly enforced. It was also one that he believed was an important key to his success in the freighting business. In his memoirs, *Seventy Years on the Frontier*, Majors made the connection between his pious policies and his life's achievement in the freighting business, noting:

> I could not have formulated a better code of rules for the government of my business than those adopted, looking entirely from a moral standpoint. The results proved to be worth more to me [financially] than that resulting from any other course I could have pursued, for with the enforcement of these rules . . . gave me control of the business of the plains and, of course, a wide-spread reputation for conducting business [with] a humane plan.***

Perhaps Majors's employees of the trail did not balk at his religious requests because they appreciated his own behavior while on a freighting run. Majors did not lord over his workers, even after he had become a wealthy man. Unlike William Russell, who operated his freighting businesses from an office, Majors remained on the trail, often walking alongside an ox team pulling a heavily laden wagon. He ate his meals around common campfires along with his men and, after saying his evening prayers, lay down on the ground with his bedroll under a wagon right alongside every common man in his employ.

---

* Nevin, 68.

** Waddell F. Smith, ed., *The Story of the Pony Express* (San Francisco: Hesperian House, 1960), 65.

*** DiCerto, 35.

(continued from page 41)

expectations. (For example, the 1858 contract to supply forts in Utah alone amounted to delivering 16 million pounds [7.2 million kg] of freight, which required 3,500 wagons.)

To form such a company and to eliminate competition from Alexander Majors, Russell and Waddell struck up a partnership with their rival, resulting in the largest freighting company in the West, one that could probably monopolize regional freighting and government contracts. The agreement was signed on December 28, 1854, creating the new firm of Russell, Majors & Waddell. The trio of entrepreneurs based their new firm in Leavenworth, Kansas, which was larger than Lexington, Missouri. The three businessmen also established a new system by which they were to be paid per 100 pounds (45 kg) per mile, instead of by the total weight of the supplies or goods they were to ship.

Throughout the remainder of the 1850s, the giant freight company did not consistently make a profit. In 1857, Mormon militia units attacked and burned some of the company's freight caravans. Winter weather struck several wagon trains more, all resulting in company losses of close to $500,000. In 1858, however, the company posted a $300,000 profit. (Russell was also involved in freighting ventures on his own, looking to establish freight lines out to the Colorado gold camps around Pike's Peak. In the process, he helped establish the town of Denver as a depot site for freight wagons.) That year, the firm agreed to haul as much as 25 million pounds (11.3 million kg) of freight, while operating rolling stock amounting to 3,500 wagons, requiring a herd of 40,000 oxen. Overall, the profits made by Russell, Majors & Waddell, as well as their practical freighting experience, helped prepare the company in establishing the Pony Express.

Creating the
Pony Express

In January 1860, when William Russell promised to use the resources of the Russell, Majors & Waddell firm to establish an express mail line across the West, the government put him on a short leash, giving him only three months to get the line up and running—literally. The three partners soon moved quickly, establishing another company, the Central Overland California & Pike's Peak Express Company (COC).

A COSTLY VENTURE

They then sunk money into purchasing other express and stage companies to gain access to their routes, including the Hockaday Stage Line, which was already carrying the mail from St. Joseph to Salt Lake City through Fort Kearny, Fort Laramie, and Denver. That single purchase cost Russell $120,000 in promissory notes. Russell also bought out George

Chorpenning's line between the Mormon capital and Placerville, California, outside Sacramento. Through such purchases and buy-outs, the COC picked up several stations between St. Joseph and Salt Lake City. There were 15 stagecoach stations between St. Joseph and Julesburg, Colorado—each about 25 or 30 miles (45 km) apart—that could be converted to Pony Express stops. Out in the Far West, Chorpenning's old line included a dozen or so stage stops. New stations still had to be built, though, since existing stagecoach stops were spaced farther apart than Pony Express stations needed to be built.

While Russell made deals and returned to Washington to coordinate with politicians and bankers over the new venture, others were also at work on behalf of the company. Several other associates of Russell's were out in Salt Lake City and Leavenworth, advertising for horses for the line. John Jones ran an advertisement in a Leavenworth newspaper for 200 mares, "warranted sound, not to exceed 15 hands high, well broke to the saddle."[1] Many of the needed horses came from Army stock at the local fort. Up and down the future line, agents for the COC bought 500 horses, sometimes paying as much as $200 for each, four times the usual rate. At some locations along the trail, former stagecoach horses were bought, due to their already tested "speed, stamina, and reliability."[2] These 500 horses cost the company $87,000.

Sometimes the horses purchased were not exactly ready for the rigors of the Pony Express. Some were not really broken for riding, much less for the trail. Some had been rounded up and merely corralled before purchase. In some instances, "if a hostler could lead a mustang out of the stable without getting his head kicked off, the horse was [considered] ready to ride."[3] Just shoeing such an animal was a true task, with blacksmiths forced to tie down each of the horse's legs before beginning the shoeing process. Overall, however, the horses bought for the Pony Express were good, sturdy animals. Many came from

California, while others were purchased from horse farms in Kentucky.

Once horses were actually broken and ready to ride, they were treated well by the company, because they were an important investment. These animals were fed high-quality grain that provided them with greater strength and stamina. This was important on the trail, not only to cover ground at a high speed, but also to escape from the occasional attack. Since American Indian ponies were often inferior and fed less, "a Pony rider could always outdistance his attackers."[4] Pony Express men believed the difference was essentially that their mounts were grain-fed, while the American Indian ponies were grass-fed. Riders would also often speak of the intelligence and incredible sense of direction of Pony Express horses and their ability to keep to a trail. How much these claims were true or simply fond bragging is uncertain, but cases were documented when Pony Express mounts were able to find a rugged trail and stay on it, even in poor weather.

ESTABLISHING THE LINE

The task of setting up the physical line—including the relay stations and corrals—fell to Benjamin Ficklin, who had been serving as the general superintendent of Russell, Majors & Waddell. Ficklin had first proposed a horse-run mail line back in the early 1850s. As the newly appointed field manager for the COC, he worked with five division superintendents who were responsible for various regions along the intended trail. They supervised the construction of new relay stations and the renovation of old stage stops. Russell had calculated a need for 190 such stations, including 25 "home" stops where riders would be replaced, and 165 "swing" stops where riders would switch to fresh horses. Contracts were written with local merchants (if there were any towns close to a given relay station) to provide supplies once the stations were manned.

The relay system of the Pony Express greatly depended on the stations that were placed along the delivery routes. At these stops, horses and men could be replaced to allow tired riders and animals to rest without any gaps in service. Above, a painting entitled *The Coming and Going of the Pony Express* shows an exchange station during the winter.

As field agents established the sites for relay stations along the Pony Express route, they used only one consideration: how much ground a horse could cover at a full gallop, given the local terrain, before tiring and needing to be replaced. Everything else was secondary, which caused some problems at some stations. If a station was built at a site that had no local water supply, water had to be shipped in like all other supplies. Each station was constructed out of the locally available materials, which caused them to vary in quality and construction. If there was local timber, a wooden station was built. Across much of Nebraska, some stations were constructed of sod. Across desert lands, adobe bricks were used. In especially barren places, swing stations were built "by gouging a cavity in a hillside and roofing it over with logs hauled in from elsewhere."[5] Nearly all relay stations were built with no frills. Even "home" stations, which housed several riders, were nothing more than one-room accommodations, consisting of bunks and basic kitchen setups.

The decision was made early to establish the Pony Express route to follow, more or less, the old Oregon Trail or Pioneer Trail, which had already delivered hundreds of thousands of immigrants across the western plains and the mountain passes to Oregon and California. This would mean starting the line at St. Joseph, Missouri, and running it across Kansas, Nebraska, Colorado, Wyoming, Utah, and Nevada, with the terminus in the West in San Francisco. In all, the route would cover 1,840 miles (3,000 km). Some Leavenworth townspeople were surprised when the decision was announced to anchor the eastern end of the Pony Express in St. Joseph. After all, Leavenworth was the headquarters of Russell, Majors & Waddell. Assuming too much, prior to the announcement about St. Joseph, the *Leavenworth Daily Times* ran the banners:

GREAT EXPRESS ADVENTURE FROM
LEAVENWORTH TO SACRAMENTO IN TEN DAYS.
CLEAR THE TRACK AND LET
THE PONY COME THROUGH.

HIRING THE RIDERS

The selection of good horses was essential to the plan to deliver mail across the West in 10 days, and so was the hiring of the riders. Each division superintendent was responsible for hiring 70 to 80 riders. Typically, they looked for young men, as young as teenagers, who were highly experienced horsemen. They also sought riders who had personal stamina and were willing to face the challenges of the trails in the West, including the possibility of American Indian attacks. When recruiting riders out in San Francisco, the regional division superintendent is alleged to have placed the following advertisement:

WANTED
—young, skinny, wiry fellows, not over eighteen.
Must be expert rider, willing to risk death daily.
Orphans preferred. Wages $25 a week.
Apply, Central Overland Express,
Alta Bldg., Montgomery St.[6]

According to Pony Express records, just over 200 young men were employed at one time or another as riders. When the Pony Express was in full operation, about 40 riders were typically in the saddle at the same time along the trail. Their names include many of English, Irish, or Scottish descent, as well as Germans, African Americans, and Latinos. Some names were more colorful than others, and include such nicknames as "Sawed-Off Jim," "Little Yank," "Bronco Charlie," "Deadwood Dick," "Mochila Joe," "Black Sam," "Boston Jim," "Cyclone Charlie," "Whipsaw," two men called "Irish Tom," and, the most famous, "Buffalo Bill." (James Butler "Wild Bill" Hickok, who later gained a reputation as a Wild West gunslinger, is sometimes spoken of as a Pony Express rider, but he was only employed as a stable hand.)

The skills required for Pony Express riders included more than just mastery of the horse and bravery. Riders were often recruited to ride their own local portion of the trail because they were more likely to be familiar with it. Since they would be expected to ride regardless of rain or snow, and also at night, they would need to know the terrain. This combination of abilities soon set the Pony Express apart; admirers would consider them colorful, and even heroic. Reflecting the young men's unique abilities as Pony Express riders, wages ranged between $100 and $150 per month, depending on their specific run of the route. Only top officials in the company were paid

One of the legendary figures of the Wild West, William "Buffalo Bill" Cody, was known throughout the United States for his exploits on the rough-and-tumble frontier. After leaving home at 11 years old, Buffalo Bill was already an experienced miner, frontiersman, herder, and fur trapper when he joined the Pony Express at 14 years old.

more than the riders. Those who worked the corrals and kept the stations earned salaries as low as $50 per month, as well as room and board, both of which could prove quite minimal.

The Pony Express organizers promised to run the route between St. Joseph and the West Coast in 10 days; however, the speed of this leg of a letter's transit across the country would matter little unless the mail being funneled to St. Joseph reached the Missouri town in a timely manner. To that end, Pony Express officials designated collection sites in cities that included New York, Washington, Chicago, and St. Louis. Mail on the Pacific coast was routed as quickly as possible to San Francisco.

All this required coordination and a schedule that everyone upheld, no one more than the Pony Express riders themselves. Since the Pony Express was slated to run all hours of the day and night through sun, rain, or snow, times were pre-set for the arrival of Pony Express riders along the route. After all, some mail carried by the route's riders would reach its destination sooner than a 10-day ride simply because a destination might be located somewhere short of either end of the line. The *St. Joseph Weekly* published the schedule so everyone would know how soon a letter was scheduled to arrive at each major point along the trail. Beginning in St. Joseph, a Pony Express rider was expected to reach the following locations in the amount of time noted:

- Marysville: 12 hours
- Fort Kearny: 34 hours
- Fort Laramie: 80 hours
- Fort Bridger: 108 hours
- Great Salt Lake: 124 hours
- Carson City: 188 hours
- Placerville: 226 hours
- Sacramento: 234 hours
- San Francisco: 240 hours

Through feverish planning, fast business deals, hiring on the fly, and road adaptation that lacked any serious refinement,

Russell and his associates managed to pave the way for the opening of the Pony Express on time, by April 3, 1860. They had spent a tremendous amount of money, and the three partners of Russell, Majors & Waddell had little anticipation they would ever manage a profit with the venture. Something had caused them to take on the risk and gamble; perhaps they believed it was their patriotic duty to provide the fastest possible service to deliver the U.S. mail across an ever-expanding American landscape. They were stepping out on their own with no government support, and that reality would never change. Through the entire history of the Pony Express, the U.S. government never provided financial support to the COC or issued a contract to Russell and his partners.

THE FIRST PONY EXPRESS RIDERS

On the fateful evening of April 3, 1860, when rider Johnny Fry headed off through the darkness toward Cottonwood Springs Station, the first relay station outside St. Joseph, the Pony Express was no longer a dream, but a reality. He rode his horse hard, needing to set the pace for the new mail delivery system, as the nation's attention had been focused on him and the inaugural events in St. Joseph.

In his mochila, Fry carried the first mail to be delivered from East to West by the Pony Express. It included 49 letters, several copies of newspapers from back East, and a collection of telegraph messages intended for California newspapers. The telegraph missives were actually a gimmick dreamed up by William Russell. Telegraph lines already existed between St. Joseph and Fort Kearny, Nebraska, as well as between San Francisco and Carson City, Nevada. But there were no lines between the fort and the Nevada town, so the Pony Express was conveniently filling in the distance between the two destinations along the trail. In all, the mail Fry was carrying weighed 15 pounds, paid for at the exorbitant rate of $5 per half ounce.

A critical test of the Pony Express was its first run from St. Joseph, Missouri, to Sacramento, California. The riders were expected to ride day and night, in any kind of weather, in order to adhere to a strict schedule of arrival and departure times for each station. Above, the crowd watches as a rider for the Pony Express leaves St. Joseph, Missouri, for its inaugural run.

After nearly five hours through the night, making good time across the Kansas prairie, he reached the first home station, located at Seneca, Kansas. There he would hand off the mochila to the next rider, a 16-year-old boy named Don Rising. On a fresh horse, young Rising continued the westward chain of mail delivery. On through the darkest hours of the night his horse sped, reaching Marysville, Kansas, at 8:15 on the morning of April 4. The westbound Pony Express had covered 140 miles in little more than half a day.

Fry and Rising were not the only Pony Express riders making progress along the 1,800-mile (2,900-km) route. Out in California, the first eastbound rider had left San Francisco more than an hour before Fry (the equivalent of 4 P.M. Pacific Time by today's time schedule). Just as in St. Joseph, thousands of excited well-wishers had gathered in the streets for the first send-off along the route. Outside the offices of the local newspaper, the *Alta Telegraph*, the first eastbound rider's mochila was filled with 85 letters and placed on the back of "a clean-limbed, hardy little nankeen-colored pony,"[7] its bridle festooned with a pair of small U.S. flags. (*Nankeen* was a term used at the time to refer to the dark yellow fabric imported from China.) The first California rider was James Randall, who, after managing to mount his horse from the wrong side, threw his mount into action. It galloped down the street to where a steamboat would take horse and rider as passengers upriver to Sacramento.

Randall, however, was only there for the crowd, just as was the case with Richardson riding the first Pony Express horse to the waterfront in St. Joseph to hand the mare off to Fry, the real hired rider. Randall rode the steamer to Sacramento, where it arrived at 2:45 in the morning in a heavy downpour of rain. At that early hour, almost no one was present to witness Randall hand off the mochila to the Pony Express rider William Hamilton.

Hamilton wasted no time throwing the mail pouch over his horse's saddle before riding off into the inky blackness. The rain followed him along the trail that followed the American River, but Hamilton managed to make good speed despite the weather. Changing horses at several stations, he reached the station in the foothills of the Sierra Nevada, where he handed the mochila off to the next rider, Warren Upson, the son of the editor of an important California newspaper, the *Sacramento Union*. Hamilton had been in the saddle, riding hard, for five hours.

Young Upson's ride would be a difficult one, as the trail he was assigned was rugged and rocky, taking him through heavy snow pack. The snow was so extensive it had stopped the local stagecoach run to Carson City, a run the stage had not failed to make over the previous three years. Upson, however, pressed on, reaching the relay station named Strawberry. The young rider received assistance there from the local division superintendent, who provided him with a lead of mules to use to break through the snows that lay farther ahead on the trail at the summit of the Sierra Nevada.

Even with the help of these additional animals, Upson found the going difficult and was forced several times to dismount and lead his horse by hand. As they plodded on, a hard winter wind bore down on horse and rider. The temperatures were falling, and the wind kicked up with each advancing step that Upson took. He finally reached the top of the mountain pass, where he met others facing the same harsh, wintry conditions as he. They were leading mules through the pass from the eastern side of the mountain. As one of the strangers would note later:

> The storm grew fiercer and fiercer as we went on. The flakes of snow and hail were blowing into our faces with such power that they stung like needles, and nearly blinded us. ... On the very summit, we met a lonely rider dashing along at a tremendous rate. We wondered what could possibly induce him to go on through that gale, and thought it must be some important business. It was the Pony Express.[8]

Having crested the mountain and advanced despite the snow, cold, and wind, Upson continued down the eastern slope along a narrow and steep trail. On this, the Pony Express's maiden run, he had proven that the mail could be taken through the Sierra Nevada, despite the worst weather imaginable. As he moved down the mountainside, he left behind the storm, which was centered in the higher elevations. Here the original record is uncertain. Upson may have continued on to the first relay station across the California-Nevada border, but he may have continued on, instead, to Carson City.

That stretch of the route between Carson City and Utah's Salt Lake City would become known by Pony Express riders as a fearful part of the trail. This was due to the harshness of the land and attacks by American Indians. On this first run of the new mail system, however, American Indians were not a problem, and the difficulties of passing through the snowy summit of the Sierra Nevada faded. The mail continued to advance across the Far West under blue skies along a dry, well-worn trail. Near midnight on Saturday, April 7, a rider named Howard Egan rode into Salt Lake City with the eastbound mail. Egan was not a regular Pony Express rider, but an older district superintendent who wanted to participate directly as a rider on the Pony Express's first transcontinental run. Even though Upson had struggled through the Sierra Nevada, Egan reached the Pony Express station in the Mormon capital ahead of schedule.

COMPLETING THE FIRST RUN

By all accounts, Salt Lake City was considered the halfway mark on the trail. (In reality, the Utah community was closer to the western end of the trail rather than the middle.) Those at the station were anxious for the arrival of the westbound rider. That leg of the maiden run was running behind schedule, having been hit by poor weather conditions. The westbound horse and rider did not reach Salt Lake City until April 9. On April 8, the riders heading both east and west passed one another on the trail. How they may have greeted one another is not known. Given the tight schedule and the pressures on each rider to press on and make good time, it is unlikely that they stopped and shared a moment of history.

Following their passing, the eastbound rider continued on, making good speed since the trail beyond South Pass was fairly well defined, one worn down by years of immigrant wagon trains. Rain was a problem and portions of the trail were wet, muddy, and dangerous. But even more daunting was the Pony Express rider's crossing of the Platte River near Julesburg,

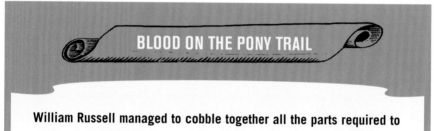

BLOOD ON THE PONY TRAIL

William Russell managed to cobble together all the parts required to create the Pony Express in a mere matter of months in early 1860. By April, the Pony Express was, as it were, up and running. With such an extensive trail system, logistical problems proved constant during the 18-month history of the Pony Express. Yet, "only once in the history of the Pony Express did the mail not go through."[*] In May 1860, just weeks after the system had begun delivering the nation's transcontinental mail, it faced one of its most trying challenges: the Paiute War. The conflict proved intense and hostile and caused the only significant disruption to Pony Express riders' ability to deliver mail in the West.

Through the winter of 1859 to 1860, the 6,000 members of the Paiute in Nevada had struggled, "freezing and starving to death by the scores," as one newspaper described their plight.[**] Many Paiute blamed white settlers for this, especially the settlers' practice of cutting down pinon trees. These trees had traditionally supplied the Paiute with nuts, an important part of their diet. In addition to this, Paiute warriors were rightly incensed after receiving word that men

Colorado; the river was running high due to the rains. The rider entered the swollen current in front of well-wishers gathered on the river's opposite bank. The current caught the horse off guard, causing the animal to lose its footing in the swift and shifting waters. With little time to respond, the rider leaped from the horse, grabbing the mochila and its precious cargo and fought his way to shore. The crowd wasted no time providing the rider with a new mount and cheered as he rode

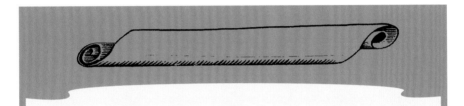

at the Pony Express's Williams Station had kidnapped and raped two Paiute women.

A respected Paiute chief named Numaga encouraged his people not to take the path of war. Despite those admonitions, Paiute warriors attacked Williams Station in Nevada on May 7 and killed five Pony Express employees, an event later referred to as the Pyramid Lake Massacre. The war had begun.

It lasted for nearly a month, and the Pony Express proved a significant target. With stations located in remote sites, it was easy for Paiute warriors to swoop in and attack successfully. Through the weeks of the Paiute War, seven Pony Express stations were burned or otherwise razed. In addition, 16 employees were killed and 150 horses taken or scattered. Chief Numaga tried to bring the war to an end as quickly as possible, but it would take the U.S. Army's intervention to end the conflict. By its end, the Paiute War had brought about the deaths of 75 people, white and Paiute alike.

* Nevin, 109.
** Ibid.

off in a high gallop. As for his poor, struggling horse, it had been swept downriver, but was rescued from the raging current by the locals.

Johnny Fry, who had ridden out from St. Joseph on the evening of April 3, would play a role in delivering the mail from the West back into the frontier Missouri town. At 5 P.M. on April 13, Fry raced down the city's streets, wheeled his horse up at the Pony Express offices, and dismounted, turning in his mochila to the officials there. It was the first delivery of the mail from California and had been delivered in 9 days and 23 hours. This was an hour ahead of schedule. Just as enthusiastic crowds had come out to see the first Pony Express rider leave town to make mail delivery history, so they were again in the streets 10 days later to repeat their celebrating. This time, it was for the completion of delivery, rather than the promise. That evening, "militiamen fired their muskets into the air, the cannon boomed, and bonfires and fireworks lit the sky."[9]

Out in California, the first delivery of westbound mail by the Pony Express arrived in Sacramento just an hour off schedule. Just after 5:30 P.M. that same day, April 13, the same rider who had ridden the mail out of Sacramento 10 days before arrived at Sutter's Fort along the American River, just outside the state capital. There, a double column of nearly 100 mounted riders greeted William Hamilton, sitting astride his mustang pony. The riders paraded alongside Hamilton into Sacramento, amid the clang of local church bells and the boom of cannon fire. A crowd was gathered along both sides of the main street, and others watched from store and hotel windows. Still more onlookers were lined up along rooftops, shouting celebratory cheers. The men tossed their hats aloft and women threw their handkerchiefs into the street. Hamilton delivered his mochila to the local Pony Express offices, and the mail was removed for delivery. The last leg of the Pony Express had been completed.

When the final messenger of the Pony Express completed his leg of the trip and arrived in Sacramento, California, the awaiting crowds greeted him with cheers and celebration. Other riders delivering correspondence along the West Coast experienced similar reactions from elated people as they realized the Pony Express was a reliable and efficient mail service.

But Hamilton was not free to rest just yet; he was soon on his way to San Francisco. He rode his horse dockside along the Sacramento River and boarded the ferry. The river craft arrived in San Francisco at 12:38 A.M. to the din of church bells, fireworks, and bonfires. Despite the midnight hour, Hamilton soon found himself the center of attention as part of a parade led by a marching band and four companies of firefighters, followed by an eager throng of Californians. As the band played "See, the Conquering Hero Comes," Hamilton was swept to the offices of the *Alta Telegraph*, completing the full circle of the East-West route.

Given the late hour, it was enough fanfare for the majority of the gathered crowd. The people shouted three cheers for Hamilton and the Pony Express, and then trudged off to their homes, proud of the successful ingenuity of this new mail system. The streets were soon cleared of the supportive mass of people, except for the young men in the crowd. Filled with excitement, they stayed up all night, unable to sleep "and feeling much closer than they had ever felt before to their fellow Americans in the East."[10]

A Rough
Western Road

From the maiden run of the Pony Express in April 1860, the young riders who signed on to deliver the mail across the desolate reaches of the American West became the stuff of legend. Russell's planned experiment to deliver the mail in 10 days had succeeded, and it seemed everyone in the country was talking about the mail delivery system they were soon referring to as "The Pony." In Washington, D.C., congressmen who had not invested a single dime of the government's money were excited about the success of the central route, with the southern route soon all but lost to the Confederacy. Even in Europe, French newspapers described "Le Poney Post" to their readers with excited prose. In no time at all, boys in the United States were buying dime novels featuring the heroics of Pony Express riders who were only a few years older than they.

THE GREAT ROUTE WEST

Perhaps part of the inspiration behind the legend of the Pony Express and its young riders was the fact that those who rode for "the Pony" did so across 1,840 miles (3,000 km) of often difficult terrain, which "was enough to tax the endurance of the sturdiest team of riders."[1] It crossed or at least touched eight states, present and future: Missouri, Kansas, Nebraska, Colorado, Wyoming, Utah, Nevada, and California. The topography of the route varied from the flat, remote grasslands of the Great Plains to great churning rivers fed by mountain snowmelt, to arid deserts where a man's bones could bleach in a matter of weeks, to upland country and formidable mountain ranges, including California's Sierra Nevada. Since the Pony Express ran through the calendar, riders faced weather conditions that swung between extremes, including searing temperatures reaching 120°F (49°C), wind-blown blizzards, barrages of hail and lightning, and rain and mud. This was all a constant challenge to the progress of horses and riders who were, by definition, always in a hurry to get somewhere.

A close look at the trail, beginning at St. Joseph, Missouri, and traveling westward, provides a perspective on the difficulties riders faced on practically every leg of the transcontinental route. By the early 1860s, St. Joseph was still a booming frontier town, the eastern anchor of western routes, including the Oregon Trail, Santa Fe Trail, freight routes into Kansas, and, most recently, the Pony Express.

Heading out of the home office and down the streets of St. Joseph, the Pony Express rider went first to the paddle-wheel ferry on the Missouri River to Elwood, Kansas, the true starting point of the mail route. Crossing northeastern Kansas, the rider found a landscape of "rolling hills, ridges, and valleys, not very difficult for a horse and rider to gallop along at a good clip."[2] In time, the rider reached an area north of the Flint Hills, noted as one of the most beautiful of the great prairie lands. In the spring, the land was covered with a carpet of wildflowers, but the prairie grass could be a problem, growing to a height of 8 feet (2.5 meters) in some places. The plains were also home to a variety of wild animals, including bison, white-tailed deer, prairie chicken, wild turkey, and prairie dogs.

Close to 100 miles (160 km) west of St. Joseph, the route reached the banks of the Big Blue River. Ahead was countryside a bit more barren than the land the rider had just crossed. It was rugged, with jagged rock features breaking the landscape. Fording the Big Blue, especially in spring when the river was swollen with whirlpools and rapids, could be life threatening. Some historians believe a ferry was in operation across the Big Blue at the time of the Pony Express, which would have made a river crossing much easier. After making the crossing, the rider would reach the relay station at Marysville, Kansas.

Beyond the Big Blue River, the rider rode westward to the valley of the Little Blue River. He followed the river along its eastern bank as it spread out to the north, leading out of Kansas and into Nebraska. Here, the rider entered a flat stretch of land, leaving the Little Blue, crossing Thirty-Two Mile Creek, and reaching the valley of Nebraska's most important interior river: the Platte. The Platte River then set the rider's course for several hundred miles. Generally, a rider followed the river's south bank. The Platte is a long, meandering, and shallow river, once described as "a thousand miles long and six inches deep."[3] It had served for decades to mark the trail to the West for wagon trains. A westbound rider followed the watery route against its current, as the river actually flowed eastward.

The rider stuck to the Platte, since the river provided water and abundant grass for horse forage, until he reached Fort Kearny and Midway Station. At Fort Kearny, the Pony Express mirrored the old route of the Oregon Trail and would do so across Wyoming all the way to Fort Bridger. From Midway Station, the rider rode on to Cold Springs Station. Here, in western Nebraska, the two sources of the Platte—the North Platte and the South Platte—joined together at a site near Fort

McPherson. Taking the South Platte and following it for about 100 miles (160 km), the rider turned toward the southwest and into modern-day northeastern Colorado. Here, the rider could see for miles in any direction, for he had ridden "into a land where the deep blue sky rarely blessed the earth with rain and the horizon was a nearly perfect straight line."[4] This did not last for long, as today's Colorado played a limited host to the Pony Express rider. He left the banks of the South Platte after crossing the river at Julesburg, and turned toward the northwest, back into Nebraska and its western panhandle.

BEYOND THE MOUNTAINS

Although the Rocky Mountains still lay in the remote distance, the Pony Express rider began to experience a more difficult and rugged terrain. In this desolate country, "the land began to rise, giving way to buttes, spires, mesas, and some of nature's most startling monuments of the journey west."[5] Such notable and natural trail markers as the sandstone outcroppings of Courthouse Rock and Jail House Rock could be seen from miles away. Next, the rider reached Chimney Rock, a favorite of Oregon Trail immigrants, followed by a steep ridge called Scotts Bluff and a break in the ridge, Mitchell Pass, which offered a welcome opening. Not far after passing these natural formations, the rider finally bade good-bye to Nebraska and entered Wyoming, with its mighty mountains ahead. Fort Laramie lay in the distance, but was still 80 miles (130 km) away.

Upon exiting Mitchell Pass, the trail began to rise into new country, the Wyoming foothills of the Rockies. The rider had to cross a myriad of coldwater streams, even as his horse continued to climb the trail that had slowly been rising to a height of 7,000 feet (2,100 meters) above sea level over the past several hundred miles of trail. Once past Fort Laramie, the rider followed the trail up and down foothills for 150 miles (240 km) until another natural landmark rose into view just to the north. It was a gray, granite outcropping nearly 200 feet (60 m)

Delivery routes often ran through some of the most beautiful natural land-scapes in the United States, like Red Rock Canyon in Wyoming. Though scenic, riders needed to be focused and tough to endure the extreme heat during the day and the freezing cold of night while staying on schedule.

high, which immigrants called Independence Rock. Those who passed this site on the Oregon Trail came to call the rock the "Great Register of the Desert," since many left the trail to carve their names onto the massive turtle shell–shaped stone. Pony Express riders, of course, did not take the time to leave the trail and autograph the rock. They were on a schedule.

Just a few miles beyond Independence Rock, the rider reached Devil's Gate, a narrow defile in a cliff wall 300 feet high, which opened a path to the Sweetwater River. The rider followed this stream for 100 miles (160 km) before arriving at South Pass, a wide opening in the Rocky Mountains. The pass lay in the center of the southwest quadrant of modern-day Wyoming. Here, the rider crossed the Continental Divide, the topographical spine of the great Rocky Mountains chain. Flanked by the Sweetwater Mountains and Antelope Hills to the south, and the Rattlesnake Mountains and Wind River Range on the north side, South Pass marked the highest elevation the rider would reach in his quest to deliver the mail from the Midwest to the Pacific Coast.

Once through the great mountain pass, the rider turned to the southwest, following Sandy Creek "down along the butter-colored banks of the swiftly running Green River, into Utah Territory."[6] Although he had found his way through the formidable Rocky Mountains, which offered travelers everything from high winds to heavy snow, the rider soon faced some of the worst terrain and conditions of the trail. Ahead were hundreds of miles of desolate and lonely desert. Here the previously abundant game and wildlife petered out, and salt flats spread out in the rider's path. There was little this region offered but alkali dust; an intense, stifling heat; and an average annual rainfall of 5 inches (13 centimeters). It is a region known as the Great Basin, due to the lack of an adequate and natural water drainage system. The desert was equally forbidding in its scope, covering nearly all of Utah, a corner fragment of southwestern Wyoming, and most of modern-day Nevada. The basin's landscape is dotted with plant life unique to the region, including creosote bush, sagebrush, pinon, and juniper. For the rider, it could be a hellish place.

Those who laid out the Pony Express route fortunately did not place it across the main stretch of the salt flats. They wisely chose a path that arrived in Utah just east of the Valley of the Great Salt Lake. It then continued on to Salt Lake City, where a home station was established. Beyond the Mormon capital, the rider pointed his horse south, toward Utah Lake, and then to the west toward the Topaz Mountains, just slipping along the edge of the forbidding salt flats, "a deposit of a billion tons of salt left by a prehistoric twenty-thousand-square-mile lake."[7]

Then, the trail turned northwest through the Deer Creek Mountains into Nevada Territory, following a nearly string-straight line across the bleak landscape. The path stayed far south of the Humboldt River, which had been used for two decades by immigrant wagon trains following the California Trail. So hostile and desolate was this region that a trail through it had not even been established until 1858, just two years before the startup of the Pony Express. That route had been the work of a U.S. Army explorer, Captain James Simpson, who blazed the path between Salt Lake City and Carson Sink. The Simpson route was essential for the Pony Express. The old Humboldt-based trail used by wagon trains measured more than 850 miles (1,370 km), while the Simpson trail line was nearly 300 miles (480 km) shorter.

At Nevada's Carson Sink, the rider continued on through one of the most forbidding sections of the trail, where "dust storms could blot out the sun and tear at a rider's skin like sandpaper."[8] Past the sink, the path would soon be blocked by the great rise of the Sierra Nevada. The mountain chain was 400 miles (645 km) long and had few breaks or passes, so the rider rode toward the sky to Carson Pass, standing sentinel over the beautiful, tree-lined Lake Tahoe.

Once through the pass, however, the desert loomed ahead again as the trail reached toward California. Although the desert featured climatic extremes of hot days and freezing nights, the rider knew he would soon close the gap between St. Joseph—more than 1,800 miles (2,900 km) behind him now—and the state capital. Passing through prospecting settlements such as Placerville and Folsom, the intrepid rider soon reached the American River, where gold had been discovered in 1848. He then went on to Sacramento. Although San Francisco was the official end of the line for the Pony Express, Sacramento marked the end of the rider's time in the saddle. He would now take passage on a steamer on the swiftly moving Sacramento River to the salty waters of San Francisco Bay.

With a trail as formidable as that laid out by officials of the Pony Express, it is no wonder the mail line drew riders from among the hardiest found in the West. When they signed on with the company to become Pony Express riders, young men were agreeing to live rough lives with few amenities, put in long hours in the saddle, and brave everything the trail had to offer, from storms and wild animals to unfriendly American Indians to bandits. They lived in stark relay stations, subsisting on diets of beans, bacon, cornbread, and black coffee.

During a tour of the American West of 1860, world traveler Sir Richard Burton visited Pony Express stations between Salt Lake City and Sacramento. He observed:

> On this line there are two kinds of stations, the mail stations, where there is an agent in charge of five or six "boys," and the express station . . . where there is only a master and an express rider . . . It is a hard life, setting aside the chance of death—no less than three murders have been committed by the Indians during this year—the work is severe; the diet is sometimes reduced to wolf-mutton, or a little boiled wheat and rye, and the drink to brackish water; a pound of tea comes occasionally, but the droughty souls are always "out" of whiskey and tobacco.[9]

(Despite Burton's reference to alcohol, officially Pony Express riders were not allowed to drink.)

Pony Express stations varied dramatically in style and comfort. The more remotely they were located, the more primitive they usually were. The absolute worst were shacks with dirt floors and no glass in the windows. Bunks were built along the walls and interior furniture might be little more than benches and old boxes that had been used to ship supplies to the station. A station might be "decorated" with equipment and tools, including axes, hammers, saws, brooms, tin plates, buckets, blankets, scissors, candles, matches, and other items. Housekeeping was equally crude. The station's adjacent stable might be no better or worse than the station itself. Typical equipment found there included an assortment of horse tack—bridles, rope, and blankets—along with blacksmith supplies. Brushes and currycombs for the horses were necessary, as were manure forks.

RIDERS FOR THE PONY

Those who signed up to be riders formed a varied cast of young men from a wide variety of backgrounds, from conservative Christians to those who were skirting the law on a regular basis. In his book *Orphans Preferred*, historian Christopher Corbett profiles some of those who formed the Pony Express rosters:

> The employees of the firm were a merry mix of men. On the eastern end of the line . . . were riders like Johnny Frey [also Fry or Frye], a Kansan who had grown up in the saddle on a ranch in the eastern part of the state and was famous around the countryside as a horse racer. Along the middle section of the route, in western Nebraska, the firm hired Joseph Slade to oversee operations. Slade, a notorious desperado whom Mark Twain vividly describes in *Roughing It*, was a famous badman on the frontier, later lynched by vigilantes in Montana. And elsewhere down the line, Russell, Majors & Waddell hired Mormon farm boys, born in the saddle and familiar with the rough country they would have to cross in the wilds of Nevada and Utah.[10]

Those hired were typically young, in their early twenties or even their late teens. Company officials also considered an applicant's height and weight before a young man was signed on. The shorter and lighter a boy was, the better his chances of

In order to maintain their reputation for speedy delivery, the Pony Express preferred to hire young men who would not slow the horses down with excess weight. These men needed to be familiar with horse riding and also tough enough to endure the harsh climates of the Rocky Mountains and the southwest region. Above, riders for the Pony Express pose for a portrait.

getting a job as a Pony Express rider. Although the mail line's schedule was based on riders covering 8 to 10 miles per hour (13 to 16 kilometers per hour) on average, on some stretches they had to ride 20 miles per hour (32 kph). At that speed, a horse needed to be carrying a light load. Even the weight of the mail was regulated. In his memoirs, Majors recalled that a single mochila's mail was not to exceed 10 pounds (4.5 kg).

One of the few incentives for joining the Pony Express was the relatively good pay. Riders might receive as much as $150 per month, decent wages, considering a typical young man on the frontier might hire out for work at a dollar a day. Even skilled workers, such as blacksmiths or carpenters, might receive $3 a day for their labors. Given the risks, however, the money was actually inadequate. Rider Nick Wilson recalled: "Our pay was too small for the hard work and the dangers we went through."[11] In addition, the company did not provide everything for a rider and would charge the rider for such necessities as a saddle and even the company-issued revolver. A rider's first wages might be held back to cover the cost of such trail essentials.

There were no official Pony Express uniforms; riders wore whatever clothing worked for them, so costumes among the boys varied. Typically, though, they might wear a hunting shirt made of buckskin, or else a red flannel shirt, along with heavy cloth or felt pants, high boots, and a slouch hat or jockey cap. They were to carry nothing personal, just what they needed, which included weapons. Author Mark Twain described the young men as "flying light."[12] Originally, the riders were issued a Spencer or Sharps rifle and a pair of Colt revolvers, but this arsenal was soon reduced to a single Colt pistol with a second cylinder of ammunition also provided. In the beginning, the riders also carried horns to announce their arrival at a station, but these were soon considered unnecessary, too.

Their training was skeletal, but the company's imperative was clear: Under no circumstances was the mail ever to stop once it departed on horseback from Sacramento or St. Joseph. *Keep moving* was the mantra. The elements—whether snow, hail, or sandstorm—were no excuse for failing one's duty. As one rider later recalled: "When we started out we were not to turn back, no matter what happened, until we had delivered the mail at the next station. We must be ready to start back at half a minute's notice, day or night, rain or shine, Indians or no Indians."[13] Discipline was strict for those waiting in relay stations for the next rider to come their way. A young Mormon rider named Nick Wilson, who would later settle among the Shoshone, remembered how he and others "had to go before a justice of the peace and swear we would be at our post at all times, and not go farther than one hundred yards from the station except when carrying the mail."[14]

Everyone involved in the Pony Express, from company officials to the riders in the field, understood that speed was the key to the scheme's ultimate success or failure. Company policy and the route's schedule allowed for riders to take two minutes at each station to change horses and return to breakneck speed, but most changes took less than 30 seconds. Those living at each station knew the schedule and knew when a rider was generally due to arrive. They were expected to have the relief horse ready and saddled so that the incoming rider only had to swing down from his mount, remove the mochila, place it on his fresh horse, and remount.

With speed so important, riders were instructed to avoid all distractions, including American Indians and trail thieves, usually referred to as "road agents." After all, riders had a particular advantage when encountering a menace on the trail: Pony Express horses were the best stock and had been purchased for their speed and endurance. Riders were simply expected to keep to the trail and outrun anything that gave chase. Their horses allowed them to escape from danger and keep to their schedule, so keeping the horses fresh was essential. Riders changed mounts an average of every 12 to 15 miles (20 to 25 km), depending on the difficulty of the local terrain. A rider might stay in the saddle for 75 to 100 miles (120 to 160 km) before another rider relieved him.

AN EXPENSIVE SERVICE

Pony Express mail was expensive. Because the price was originally set at $5 per half ounce, the line riders were usually carrying important pieces of mail—communications considered worth the price. (In April 1861, after a year in operation and losing money daily, the Pony Express dropped the half-ounce rate to $2.) About two of every three pieces of mail carried by the Pony Express took the form of business communications and newspapers. More mail was delivered from California heading east than from St. Joseph heading west. Perhaps Californians felt a greater sense of isolation from the rest of the country. Some supporters of the Pony Express believed that if the amount of mail sent to the West had been equal to that sent to the East, the mail service might have been able to stay in business much longer and maybe even make a profit.

Other important mail carried by the Pony Express included telegrams. Riders commonly connected the distance between the farthest advances of the telegraph system in the West. Telegrams were often picked up at Fort Kearny in the East and Carson City in the West, since telegraph lines ran to both locations.

Government mail was also frequent and included communications sent by foreign powers. European diplomats stationed in Asia could send messages to their native countries faster through the Pony Express than they could if they relied on steamships traveling around South America or across Panama. In 1860, when the British Empire went to war with the Chinese, the government in London used the Pony Express to deliver official communications from England to the Far East. They reportedly paid as much as $135 for the delivery of some of their most sensitive documents.

To pay as little as possible, senders often wrote their messages on thin tissue paper and wrapped them in oilcloth. (Standard letter envelopes were not yet readily available.) Pony Express rider Henry Inman remembered nearly 40 years later: "There were no silly love missives among them nor frivolous correspondence of any kind: business letters only that demanded the most rapid transit possible and warranted the

THE PONY EXPRESS'S UNIQUE MAIL POUCH

One of the most unique pieces of Pony Express equipment was the mochila, or mail pouch. It was placed over a specially designed Pony Express saddle. Since an ordinary saddle weighed so much, a stripped-down model was needed. It included a shortened skirt and stirrups, a short horn in front, and a low cantle at the back of the rider's seat. It was likely patterned after the typical jockey saddle of that period. It is not clear who the designer of this special saddle was, but the St. Joseph saddle maker Israel Landis is known to have fashioned several for westbound Pony Express riders. Landis also crafted the special mail pouches.

The mochila was a rectangular piece of leather about one-eighth of an inch thick (0.3 cm) that featured a pair of slits to accommodate the unique Pony Express saddle with its specially designed horn and cantle. The leather pouch was slipped over the saddle during each run. A mochila included four leather pockets, called *cantinas*, which were placed at the mochila's four corners. It was latched closed and secured with small locks; station keepers at both ends of the Pony Express line had keys that opened three of the cantinas. Along the route, new mail picked up between Sacramento and St. Joseph was placed in the fourth cantina.

immense expense attending their journey, found their way by the Pony Express."[15]

In the beginning, the amount of mail carried by the Pony Express was a mere trickle. The cost was considered prohibitive. In time, though, the mail service became more popular. After six months in operation, Pony Express riders were carrying about 41 letters on average per ride from back East to San

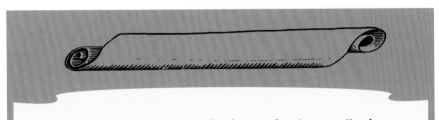

The rider **Nick Wilson** wrote in his memoirs clear recollections about the typical mochila:

Two large pieces of leather about sixteen inches wide by twenty-four long were laced together with a strong leather string thrown over the saddle. Fastened to these were four pockets, two in front and two behind; these hung on each side of the saddle. The two hind ones were the largest. The one in front on the left side was called the "way pocket." When the express arrived at the home station, the keeper would unlock the "way pocket" and if there were any letters for the boys between the home stations, the rider would distribute them as he went along. There was also a card in the way pocket that the station keeper would take out and write on it the time the express arrived and left his station.[*]

Both the special saddle and the mochila proved serviceable for the Pony Express. Since weight was such an important consideration to the speed of the horses and riders, it was vital that both the saddle and the mochila weighed only 13 pounds (5.9 kg) total, much less than a conventional saddle.

*Corbett, 87.

Francisco. By October 1861, near the end of the Pony Express's history, the average number per ride had more than doubled, to 90. These numbers may, in fact, be low estimates. Pony Express rider William Campbell recalled carrying as many as 250 letters in a single run. When the end of the Pony Express was near, riders were carrying about 350 letters per ride, according to the chief postal clerk in Atchison, Kansas, which served as the mail line's eastern anchor during the service's last few months. Through its entire history, the Pony Express successfully delivered nearly 35,000 pieces of mail.

"The Lonesomest Kind of Job"

Possibly every man, woman, and child in the United States was aware of the unique work of the Pony Express riders. Even as the shadow of the approaching Civil War drew long in April 1861, stories of the undaunted Pony Express riders were still splashed across the front pages of newspapers nationwide. They caught the imagination of the old and young alike, and they were often admired by young ladies inspired by the dash and courage of the equally young riders. Rider Johnny Fry "so charmed the girls along his route that they were said to wait by the wayside to proffer cakes and cookies they had baked just for him." According to one questionable account, a young female admirer invented the doughnut "so that Johnny could spear the snack on one finger at full gallop."[1]

Excitable young female admirers aside, the work of the Pony Express rider was work done alone, with only a horse as a companion. It was a labor that relied on hundreds of riders whose lives only touched one another for that brief moment when a rider reached a station and a new rider received the mochila, taking up his portion of the trail alone. It was work that one rider, Charley Cliff, called "the lonesomest kind of a job."[2]

HEROISM AND CHALLENGE

For many, the Pony Express represented heroism, young men accepting the challenge of delivering mail sent by strangers across territory that was alternately rugged, demanding, and hostile. They were intrepid riders willing to risk all, even their very lives, to keep East and West connected along a tenuous ribbon of a trail.

And they moved with lightning speed. Although most newspaper reporters never actually saw a Pony Express rider in action, some did. Among those who did was Mark Twain, known today as one of the country's greatest writers. He was traveling across the West in a stagecoach in 1861 when a Pony Express rider was spotted in the distance. Passengers cranked their heads in the rider's direction and shouted, "Here he comes!" Twain wrote about the excitement he and his fellow passengers felt as the hard-riding young man approached:

> Away across the endless dead level of the prairie a black speck appears against the sky, and it is plain that it moves. Well, I should think so! In a second or two it becomes a horse and rider, rising and falling, rising and falling—sweeping toward us nearer and nearer—growing more and more distinct, more and more sharply defined—nearer and still nearer, and the flutter of the hoofs comes faintly to the ear—another instant a whoop and a hurrah from our upper deck, a wave of the rider's hand, but no reply, and man and horse burst past our excited faces and go swinging away like a belated fragment of a storm![3]

Newspaper stories often told of the harrowing adventures riders sometimes faced, struggling against American Indian attacks and other challenges. Some stories featured descriptions of how intrepid riders covered long distances against the perils of nature, including floods and storms. Although most of the Pony Express riders would remain obscure and unknown, even nameless to most people, some would become the stuff of legend as true and authentic national heroes. As rider William Campbell reflected in his later years, he and his fellow riders had a sense they were "helping to make history."[4]

WILLIAM CAMPBELL OF NEBRASKA

Some heroes of the Pony Express are remembered better than others because they either wrote about themselves later in life, or someone else wrote their story for them. One who was interviewed later in life was William Campbell, who worked for the Pony Express when he was only 18. During his time with the service, young Campbell "faced just about every difficulty one could imagine on the trail."[5]

Born in 1842 in frontier Illinois, Campbell went West at age 16 with his brother, and the two young men took jobs with Russell, Majors & Waddell as bullwhackers accompanying freight wagons on the Santa Fe Trail. Their pay was $25 per month. Campbell would later in life explain the difference between the Pony Express and his earlier work experience: "Driving slow oxen seemed pretty tame compared with jumping on spirited ponies and going full tilt along the old trail, past the emigrant trains and freight outfits, or even bands of Indians."[6] Yet freighting had its adventures, including a day when a group of Pawnee stampeded a herd of bison into Campbell's wagon train.

By the early months of 1860, company men tapped young Campbell to help build and supply relay stations east of Salt Lake City for the new Pony Express. Seeing the new riders with their high spirits and dashing horses convinced Campbell that he, too, wanted to become one. At first, Alexander Majors refused. Campbell weighed 140 pounds and was 6 feet tall (63.5 kg at 1.8 m), too heavy and too tall by the preferred standards for riders. By late 1860, however, after eight months running, the company was having trouble recruiting new riders. Majors then hired Campbell.

In no time, Campbell realized the difficulties of carrying the mail. His first run route was between Nebraska's Fort Kearny and Fort McPherson at Plum Creek, a distance of 100 miles (160 km). During one run, his horse, Ragged Jim, galloped into a muddy buffalo wallow, sending Campbell and his mochila flying over his horse's head. His mount, confused, lost direction and went galloping back the wrong way, leaving Campbell stranded. Fortunately, a stagecoach passed nearby, caught the horse, and then found Campbell walking along with his mochila. With horse and rider reunited, the two then returned to the trail, headed in the right direction, and raced to make up for lost time.

Such a story was actually little more than a mishap. Other Campbell adventures were more serious. During a night ride, Campbell rode upon a pack of wolves along the trail devouring a dead horse. The pack's attention was caught by the blur riding swiftly by, and it chose to give chase. Campbell had chosen the wrong time not to bring along his revolver. As the wolves moved in closer to Campbell and his horse, the young rider thought to blow his Pony Express horn, which startled the animals, causing them to temporarily stop in their tracks. But they only took up their chase again. Campbell repeatedly blew his horn, causing the wolves to fall back. Only when the lights of the next relay station shone in the distance did the wild animals finally give up their pursuit.

The weather caused some of young Campbell's most harrowing experiences. Winter weather could stop a rider in his tracks and deliver death along the remote reaches of the trail.

Snow was a constant bane. In an interview conducted more than 70 years after the days of the Pony Express, the 90-year-old Campbell, who had become a state senator in his adult years, recalled: "Once I spent twenty-four hours in the saddle carrying the mail 120 miles to Fairfield with snow two or three feet deep and the mercury around zero. I could tell where the trail lay only by watching the tall weeds on either side and often had to get off and lead my horse. There was no rider to go on at Fort Kearny, so I went on to Fairfield twenty miles away."[7] Plenty more of Campbell's rides were through menacing snowstorms. One such blizzard resulted in snow piles 3 feet deep (about 1 m) and snowdrifts above his head at some spots along the trail. "It was hard work for my brave horses to wallow through some of them," Campbell recalled. "At night I just had to trust the instinct of the horses. We couldn't make more than five miles an hour on that run."[8]

Another rider who faced the harsh adventures of the Pony Express trail was Richard Cleve, who also rode between Nebraska stations—from Midway Station to near Fort Kearney, a distance of 75 miles (120 km). During an interview in his later years, Cleve told of a ride he had made in either late January or early February 1861. All around him, a blizzard howled; the storm was so severe "there had been no Pony Express or stages from the East for four or five days because of waist-deep snow."[9] Cleve braved the snowstorm, leaving Midway Station and reaching the relay stop near Fort Kearny around 9 P.M. Finding his relief rider ill, Cleve returned to the trail, having already covered 75 miles (120 km) through the storm. His next station was 32 miles (50 km) away. After only a few miles out, the blizzard was so severe the rider was unable to see. "I . . . found it impossible to find the road," recalled Cleve. "I would get off the horse and look for the road, find it and mount the horse, but five yards I would lose it again."[10] For 12 straight hours, Cleve fought nature until he reached his station the following morning. The temperature stood at 40°F below zero.

Because people wrote and sent letters throughout the year, the Pony Express continued to run in the winter, through unpredictable mountain weather. Despite the potential hazards, the riders and their horses continued on the routes. Above, a depiction of a Pony Express rider braving a fierce snowstorm in the Sierra Nevada Mountains.

Since the station was a through stop, he had to push on following his breakfast. He made the 25 miles (40 km) to Liberty Farm, the next stop, despite the drifting whiteout. Then he rode another 28 miles (45 km) to Kiowa Station. Along this stretch, he passed through more than 20 deep ravines filled with snowdrifts, leading his horse along on foot. He reached his next station after dark, having put behind him another day of blizzard conditions. Again, with no rider having arrived from the East yet, Cleve doggedly pushed on to the relay station at Big Sandy, where a stock tender agreed to take the next ride. It was the replacement rider's good fortune to meet up with a westbound rider and four or five stagecoaches running in tandem. The young Cleve had been on the move for 36 hours, facing constant snows and temperatures that hovered between 35°F and 40°F below zero. Once he had passed the mail off to a replacement, Cleve did the obvious: "I went to the house as soon as the young man started with the mail. I saw a cot in the corner of the room and went for it. I believe I was asleep before I even got to it."[11] He had covered 160 miles (260 km), fighting blizzards over each mile of the trail.

HEROICS ON THE TRAIL

Another highly praised hero of the Pony Express was Nick Wilson, who began carrying the line's mail at the age of 15. Wilson was born in 1845 in Adams County, Illinois, and his family moved out to Utah when he was only five. By age seven, he was out tending sheep for his father. His family history does not explain why, but, at age 11, Wilson went to live with the Shoshone, learning their language and being taken in as the adopted son of the chief's mother. When he heard of the planned Pony Express in 1860, he wanted to join up immediately. At first, he was denied due to his age, but once he showed off his prowess on horseback, and given his intimate knowledge of American Indian life, officials agreed to hire him.

Given his background of living with the Shoshone, it is ironic that Wilson would face repeated encounters with American Indians of the West. He was stationed in his home territory, riding between Schell Creek Station and Deep Creek Station. During one ride, Wilson rode into Deep Creek Station at the end of one relay to find no replacement rider. Despite being exhausted from his completed ride, he pressed on, reaching the station at Willow Creek after two more hours on the trail. When he arrived there, he learned that American Indians had killed his replacement.

At around 4 P.M., while he was still at the station, a party of seven Indian warriors arrived and demanded some food. When the station keeper, Peter Neece, offered them a hefty sack of flour, they demanded more. After he handed them each a sack, they again refused and Neece ordered them out of his station. As the angry group rode away, they shot arrows into a lame cow in the corral. Angered, Neece fired shots at them from his two revolvers and hit two of them, knocking them from their mounts. The remaining five warriors rode off.

Knowing his actions would probably bring the men back (as well as a couple dozen more camping in a nearby canyon), Neece told Wilson and the others at the station to arm themselves with every gun in the station and hide out nearby and surprise the group when it returned, probably after nightfall. That evening, the American Indians did return. In the ensuing gun battle, young Wilson became so scared he simply hid in a ravine until the shooting stopped and several of the American Indians rode away.

Wilson continued to hide, fearing he was the only survivor. Writing years later, he recalled:

> I crouched down . . . and lay there for a long time, maybe two hours. Finally everything was very still, so I thought I would go around and see if my horse was where I had staked him, and if he was, I would go back to my station in Deep Creek

and tell them that the boys were all killed and I was the only one that had got away. Well, as I was crawling around the house on my elbows and knees, just as easily as I could, with both pistols ready, I saw a light shining between the logs in the back part of the house. I thought the house must be full of Indians.[12]

Wilson was soon surprised to discover all his comrades were still alive. They had killed five of the American Indians, and had been out looking for him.

Wilson faced other incidents with American Indians during his months with the Pony Express. During a ride not long after the above incident, four American Indians leapt out from hiding places among some boulders and attacked Wilson. He turned his animal to outrun his attackers, as instructed, but three more American Indians stood in his path and cut him off, their arrows aimed at the young rider. With nowhere to escape, Wilson appeared done for. The one-eyed leader of the party approached, demanding that the rider dismount and hand over his revolver.

With hope fading, Wilson then recognized one of the warriors, a man named Tabby, who was a former friend of his father. The boy still did not dare speak to the warrior, who did not even appear to recognize him. The leader of the party told Wilson they were no longer going to tolerate whites crossing their land on horseback, "that he and his people intended to drive out the white man, burn the stations, and kill the riders."[13] The chief then drew away and talked with his warriors for several minutes. An anxious Wilson assumed he would soon be killed.

A warrior approached and asked for tobacco, and Wilson obliged. After the men smoked, Tabby came forward and informed Wilson he would be spared. The seven warriors had voted, but the count had to be unanimous and Tabby had not agreed to young Wilson's death. Tabby warned the boy not to

The incoming droves of settlers and miners angered the American Indians who had been living in the western United States for generations. Perceiving them as trespassers, the American Indians tried to intimidate and push out the invaders with force. Pony Express riders and stations were often subject to confrontations, as some of the delivery routes ran through American Indian territory. The riders, who were usually alone with their horses, were instructed to outrun the American Indians.

ride this leg of the trail again or he would surely not receive a stay of execution a second time.

Even with this stern warning of sure death, young Wilson knew his job was to deliver the mail he had in hand. He argued with Tabby to explain the necessity to his fellow warriors. Promising he would not deliver the mail through their lands again, Wilson received approval to complete his run. True to his word, the young rider did not ride that leg of the trail again. His route was reassigned to another rider and the route was moved over into Nevada, off of the American Indians' land.

ENDLESS ADVENTURES

This would not mark the end of Wilson's brushes with American Indians. Even though these earlier encounters were hair-raising enough, his worst adventure was yet to come. During one period of Wilson's tenure with the Pony Express, regional violence between American Indians and whites reached a high point. Arriving at the Spring Valley Station during one run, he discovered that the station keeper had abandoned his post, sensing an imminent attack. Manning the station were two young brothers who had been abandoned following the deaths of their parents from cholera. Not long after Wilson's arrival, the trio of boys heard American Indians outside the station running off with the horses. All three ran out and fired their handguns at the warriors. Wilson ran ahead of the younger boys to hide behind a large cedar tree, only to receive an arrow in his face, just a couple of inches above his left eye. Wounded severely, he was unable to stop the American Indians from stealing the station's horses.

Wilson's wound needed tending, but when the boys tried to remove the arrowhead, they broke off the shaft, leaving the flint still embedded in his skull. Feeling Wilson would soon die, the boys lit out for the next Pony Express station. As for Wilson, he "lay there all night, easy prey for wolves, mountain lions, or wandering war parties."[14] The next morning, men accompanied the boys back to the station, expecting to find Wilson dead. Surprising them all, he had survived the night despite his difficult circumstances and serious wound.

A doctor was summoned from a significant distance away. He removed the arrowhead, but could do little else for the struggling boy. Even the doctor did not expect him to pull through. Wilson remained in a coma for the next six days, and for nearly a month after that he struggled to stay alive. Once he began to turn a corner and recover, however, it was only a matter of weeks before he was back in the saddle, delivering mail.

CHARLIE MILLER
(1850–1955)

The Pony Express's Youngest Rider

As a general rule, the Pony Express relied on young men, many in their late teens and early twenties, to deliver the mail across the American West. Some riders were even younger, such as 14-year-old Billy Tate. Others who rode for the Pony Express were even younger than Tate. Perhaps the youngest was a California boy who had not yet reached his teen years.

One day in July 1861, 11-year-old Charlie Miller was hanging around the Pony Express station in Sacramento when a horse arrived at full gallop, but with no rider. The station operator told the youth that American Indians had probably killed the rider. With no rider on hand, young Charlie begged the station operator to let him take the saddle and deliver the mail to the next station. He explained that he was familiar with the local countryside. In a pinch, the station operator gave the youth his chance and off Charlie went toward Placerville.

Having proven himself, Miller, who would become known as "Bronco Charlie," was hired to ride for the Pony Express. He covered the run between Carson City and Placerville until the last days of the mail service.

Although Pony Express records do include Charlie Miller as a rider, there are questions about the story of how he became a rider in the first place. His version has some faults. The horse that

His wound left him with a terrible scar and, for the rest of his life, Nick Wilson wore a hat.

Wilson lived to see the end of the Pony Express. When it went out of business, he found another job delivering mail

reached the station with no rider must have arrived from the West, from either the Benicia Station or by way of a steamboat from San Francisco. Regardless of which, that stretch was not a likely place for a rider to be killed by American Indians. Also, since Sacramento was a home station, it is extremely curious why there was not a single rider available to continue to the next station.

Also, Miller claimed he made his first run to Placerville. Since Placerville Station was just a relay station, it would not have been his final destination. That would have been Sportsman's Hall, a home station, where he would have actually been replaced. Another questionable claim was that he became a rider between Carson City and Placerville. Since this route was more than 100 miles (160 km) of difficult trail, it seems unlikely that the station operator would have assigned it to an 11-year-old boy.

Still, his name is right there in the records of the Pony Express as a rider. Some historians speculate that he may not have ridden for long with the Pony Express, but was hired only as a temporary replacement rider, which is exactly what he was on his original run. Perhaps the truth will never be completely known. If "Bronco Charlie" was 11 when he rode for the Pony Express, even if only for a short time, he was likely the youngest rider ever to run the mail line. Since he did not die until 1955, at the age of 105, he was also the last surviving Pony Express rider, as well as the oldest.

from Salt Lake City to settlements in Montana. By 1865, he married and he and his wife moved to Bloomington, Idaho. Wilson, still only in his early twenties, ran a successful general store, blacksmith shop, sawmill, and ranch there.

Although he had certainly had some bad experiences with American Indians while riding with the Pony Express, he proved himself to be a local peacemaker between whites and the native population near Bloomington. In his later years, Wilson continued to live in the West. He moved to Wyoming, where he led the first wagon train through Teton Pass. By the 1890s, he had a full life of adventure behind him. In 1893, he became a bishop in the Mormon Church. Shoshone he had known in his teen years kept contact with him, paying him visits from time to time. Wilson lived to be 70 years old and finally died in 1915 in a town named for him—Wilson, Wyoming.

Pony Riders
of Endurance

Pony Express riders never ran out of unique experiences that required a unique level of fortitude, push, and enterprise. Those most often remembered among their comrades were the riders whose exploits made for good stories around a station corral or at the end of a hard day's labor, sitting around a campfire outdoors. The work of the Pony Express riders was so difficult that the stories never ended.

One rider whose experiences became legendary was Jack Keetley, born in England in November 1841. He grew up in Marysville, Kansas, and became a Pony Express rider at age 19, continuing to serve until the mail service went out of business. Keetley rode between Marysville and Big Sandy, Nebraska. He became known for his extraordinary endurance on the trail, a quality he revealed time and again.

A HISTORIC RUN

Keetley would be remembered for one run especially. After finishing his regular Big Sandy-Marysville run, he agreed to continue carrying the mail when his replacement was unavailable for reasons unknown today. It was a leg of the trail that ran eastward to Elwood, Kansas, on the Missouri River. (Some historians believe he may have actually begun his run at Rock Creek, Nebraska, and finished at St. Joseph.) Regardless, the distance was approximately the same—200 miles (320 km).

He mounted up for his additional run without even taking time to rest, eating while riding his galloping horse. Then, once he completed his extended eastbound run, he delivered the westbound mochila to Seneca, Kansas. In all, Keetley completed a total run of 340 miles (550 km) in 31 hours, a feat he accomplished without making any extensive stops. By the time he reached the Seneca Station, he had to be lifted off his horse by the station attendant and another hand. Keetley was fast asleep in the saddle.

Another rider noted for his endurance in the saddle was 18-year-old William James, originally from Virginia, whose family had moved to Utah when he was five years old. At 17, young Billy was riding for the Pony Express between Simpson's Park and Cold Springs in Nevada, a distance of 60 miles (nearly 100 km) through Shoshone country. To cover his route, he had to pass through a desolate and remote countryside on his California mustang. Carrying the mail both ways, he had to cross two mountains, regardless of the weather. On his fastest delivery, he covered the total distance of 120 miles (193 km) in 12 hours flat.

Jim Moore was another endurance rider. In early June 1860, Moore happened to be visiting the Midway Station located along the Platte River in Nebraska. A rider came in and no regular rider was in the station awaiting delivery. Jim jumped into service, grabbing the other rider's mochila, and mounted up to cover the distance westbound across one of the longest Pony

Express routes. Keeping his horse at full tilt, Moore's mount averaged 18 miles per hour through a day of hot summer sun across the desolate reaches of southwestern Nebraska.

After covering 140 miles (225 km), he reached the Julesburg Station in the northeast corner of Colorado. There, despite his fatigue and hunger, Moore was presented with a mochila bearing important news bound for Washington, D.C. No relief riders were available and the eastbound rider had been killed the previous day. This left Moore with no choice but to mount a fresh horse and ride back over the same 140 miles he had just completed. This time, he would be traveling at night with American Indians rumored to be looking to attack.

Onward he pushed his horse, despite his personal exhaustion and hunger, for he had not yet had an opportunity for a meal. Before he completed his entire two-way run, he would ride a total of 20 horses. Moore did not leave the trail until he reached Midway Station back on the Platte. It would become his personal best on the trail, covering 280 miles (450 km) in an astounding 14 hours, 46 minutes. His ride was one of a chain of riders who delivered that important government document along the entire Pony Express route in a record eastbound run of 8 days and 9 hours.

THE LEGENDARY "PONY BOB" HASLAM

While all these riders made their mark with the Pony Express as legendary young men of grit, fortitude, and determination, few could match the legend of Robert "Pony Bob" Haslam. He rode for the service from its beginning through to its final demise. He would one day complete a run remembered as the longest and the fastest in official Pony Express history.

Little is known of Haslam's early years. Born in England in 1840, he immigrated to the United States with his parents and out to the frontier. At 20 years old, he signed on with the Pony Express. His legendary run took place beginning on May 11, 1860, just five weeks after the Pony Express's inaugural run.

He had been assigned to ride the mail across Nevada, from Friday's Station along the southwest shores of Lake Tahoe on the California-Nevada border, to Fort Churchill and Buckland's Station, a distance of 75 miles (120 km).

When he began that day's run, he could not have imagined what lay ahead for him. Young Haslam covered the 20 miles (32 km) from Friday's Station to Carson City without incident. It was there that he heard the news of the previous four days of American Indian uprisings. The region had recently experienced raids carried out by the local Paiute, and he found all the horses had been commandeered by locals who were bent on giving chase to the Paiute chief, Winnemucca, and his warriors. So, Haslam continued on to Reed's Station (also referred to sometimes as Miller's Station) expecting to receive fresh horses at the stations in between. But along the way, he rode into several abandoned stations with no replacement horses available.

Haslam had little choice but to continue on his original horse, taking the time to feed his mount first. He then coaxed his tired pony to cover the last 15 miles (24 km) to Buckland's Station, which should have been the end of his official run. At the station, Haslam found his relief rider in a panic. Young Johnny Richardson, fearful of encountering Paiute along his leg of the Pony Express route, refused to leave the station. It was "one of the few recorded cases of a Pony Express rider refusing to carry the mail."[1]

On that very day, the Pony Express's western superintendent, W.C. Marley, was paying a call at Buckland's Station. Determined to keep the mail moving, Marley offered Haslam $50 to take Richardson's run, an amount of money nearly equal to a week's wages. Haslam would have to cover 115 miles (185 km) of trail through hostile Native American territory to the home station at Smith's Creek. After only 10 minutes at Buckland's Station, Haslam was back on the road on a fresh mount, heading straight into the Pony Express's history books.

One of the American Indian tribes that attacked Pony Express riders and stations was the Paiute, a group who lived in Nevada and the southwest region of the United States. While his predecessor, Captain Truckee, forged friendships with the military and the government, Chief Winnemucca (*above*) did not trust the new strangers who were using much of the needed resources in his people's territory and wanted them to leave.

Ahead of him lay some of the trail's most desolate and barren country. Haslam hurried along through the first 35 miles (56 km) of remote trail to the Sink of Carson Station (what is labeled on some Pony Express maps as Old River Station). From there, he rode more than 37 miles (60 km) through an alkali desert, the dust choking the tired rider, to Cold Springs Station. Then, he covered another 30 miles (48 km) to Smith's Creek Station (some maps refer to it as Castle Rock). Bone tired from his phenomenal ride, he had passed through American Indian territory without violent incident. After being relieved of his mochila by his replacement rider, he crept wearily off to a bunk at the station, where he slept for 8 hours straight. He had, after all, just finished a grueling run of 190 miles (305 km) across intensely difficult Far Western territory.

The story of Haslam's record run did not stop there. He awoke from his sleep with the arrival of another westbound rider at Smith's Creek Station. With no other rider in the station, Haslam knew what he had to do. He mounted a fresh horse and began retracing the route he had just completed less than nine hours earlier. In those intervening hours, however, the trail before Haslam had already changed. Paiute had carried out additional raids along the route. When he reached Cold Springs Station, he found nothing but its burned-out frame. American Indians had killed the local station keeper and taken off with the station's stock of horses. Wary, the rider remained only long enough to water his horse. Without taking time to bury the dead station keeper, Haslam hit the trail with his horse at a renewed gallop.

All along the trail ahead, Haslam remained anxious and watchful, looking for signs of American Indians. Night fell, leaving him in the dark with the eerie desert silence punctuated by the occasional howl of distant wolves. American Indians were nothing new to Pony Bob, who had fought them on several occasions and had been wounded more than once. On one occasion, he was attacked in Utah, outran his assailants, and finished his 120-mile (190-km) run with bullet wounds to an arm and his jaw broken by an arrow.

He reached Middlegate and Westgate stations, finding them intact, and he warned each station keeper of the sights he had encountered at Cold Springs. Reaching Sand Springs, he convinced the local station keeper to abandon his post, offering to ride along with him. Haslam's caution would soon be proven right. The following morning, American Indians attacked Sand Springs Station and destroyed it. When the two Pony Express employees reached the Sink of Carson Station, they found more than a dozen local residents who had been part of a larger group of whites who had set out to find Paiute warriors and kill them before they were attacked instead. At Pyramid Lake, Paiute warriors attacked the party of 60 men and killed 46 of them. The incident had unfolded just hours before Pony Bob's arrival at the station.

Even as everyone warned him not to continue his run, Haslam still felt it his duty to deliver the mail. He had, after all, taken a pledge as a Pony Express rider, regardless of circumstances. After only an hour out of the saddle at Buckland's Station, the young rider returned to the trail, with Superintendent Marley offering to double his bonus money to $100. Haslam managed to reach Buckland's Station, but, once again, found no rider available to carry the mail on to the next station. After so long on horseback, it is nearly a miracle he had the stamina to continue. He got back on the trail and headed to Friday's Station, which would have been his regular run distance.

Pony Bob covered the 75 miles (120 km) through the Sierra Nevada, reached his home station, and set a record for Pony Express riders. By covering multiple runs both ways, he had racked up an astonishing 380 miles (612 km) in less than 40 hours, never leaving horseback for any significant length of time except for his 8-hour nap. The young Robert Haslam took his accomplishment all in stride, stating: "I was rather tired, but the excitement of the trip had braced me up to stand the journey."[2]

Pony Bob Haslam's reputation as a dedicated rider, one with an unflagging dedication to the Pony Express, became well known among his colleagues. His natural abilities as a horseman with great endurance and stamina made him the choice of riders on occasions when important messages needed delivering as fast as possible. In early November 1860, after Abraham Lincoln had been elected president of the United States, Haslam was tagged to carry the news from Fort Kearny, Nebraska, to Fort Churchill, Nevada. Coaxing his horses to maintain breakneck speed, young Haslam reached Fort Churchill, only to announce his message before anyone had the chance to read it: "Lincoln is elected! Lincoln is elected!"[3] Four months later, he delivered the text of Lincoln's inaugural address on the run between Smith's Creek to Fort Churchill, a distance of 180 miles (290 km), which he covered in just over 8 hours.

Even when the Pony Express stopped running in the fall of 1861, Haslam continued to serve as an express rider the following year for Wells, Fargo & Company. He worked out of a station with which he was familiar—Friday's Station—riding to Virginia City, Nevada, including passage through the high country of the Sierra Nevada. With the coming of the railroad, Haslam's job with Wells Fargo grew unnecessary, so he moved north to Idaho, where trains did not yet run, and covered the distance of 100 miles (160 km) between Queen's River and Owyhee River on a single horse, with no stops.

He was still working in Idaho during the Modoc uprising. During one ride, he came upon the bodies of 90 Chinese workers who had been massacred by Modoc warriors. The sight sobered him enough that he made the decision to quit express riding. It proved a fortunate career choice, for his replacement rider was killed on his first run. Over the decades that followed, Haslam still worked for Wells Fargo, but as a

One of the fastest messages ever relayed through the Pony Express was the announcement of Abraham Lincoln's win in his first presidential election. A rider and his horse, both decorated with ribbons, raced across the United States delivering the message, "Lincoln is elected, Lincoln is elected!" Above, this handwritten message of Lincoln's victory was carried from Nebraska to San Francisco in a mere five days.

stagecoach driver between Salt Lake City and Denver. A true denizen of the West and an authentic American hero, Pony Bob Haslam died in Chicago in 1912 at the age of 72.

DETERMINED RIDERS

There were other notable, dutiful, and heroic riders for the Pony Express through its short history, including 21-year-old Billy Fisher, who rode out in Nevada between the Ruby Valley and Schell Creek Station, where Peter Neece was station supervisor. The young rider was once caught in a blizzard, spending 20 hours in the saddle and nearly freezing to death. He only narrowly managed to get the mail through. He was

(continues on page 104)

WILLIAM CODY
(1846–1917)

The Pony Express Exploits
of Buffalo Bill

Despite the heroics and determination of several Pony Express riders, each determined to see the mail through against overwhelming odds, none is more famous than the legendary western hero William Cody, better known as Buffalo Bill. Through his decades in the West, he experienced remarkable adventures, having "survived a starvation winter at Fort Bridger, skirmished with some American Indians and befriended others, prospected for gold in Colorado, and trapped beaver on the Plains."*

By the late nineteenth century, he had become one of the most famous men in the West and was advertising himself and the West he had grown up with through an extremely popular arena entertainment show called Buffalo Bill's Wild West Show. He was personally at center stage. His biography had made the pages of cheap, popular "dime novels" even as early as the 1870s. (His first life story was published in 1879, four years before he started his Wild West show.) But Cody's story of himself was sometimes exaggerated. Even the claims he made about his service with the Pony Express may have been less than accurate.

William Frederick Cody was born on February 26, 1846, in a log cabin near Le Claire, Iowa. His family moved to Kansas when he was eight years old, at a time when the western territory was racked by violence over the expansion of slavery. After his father died in 1857, young Will Cody took a job as a messenger for the freight company Majors and Russell (which would later add Waddell as a partner). He was paid $25 a month and rode between company wagon trains on a gray mule. The boy was only 10 years old.

When the Pony Express was organized, he was hired as a rider at the age of 14, even though his mother feared the hard work would kill him. Cody wrote of her fears in his autobiography: "She was right about this, as fifteen miles an hour on horseback would, in a short time, shake any man 'all to pieces'; and there were but very few, if any, riders who could stand it for a great length of time."[**]

His assigned run was the 116 miles (187 km) of trail between Red Buttes on the North Platte River to the Three Crossings Station on the Sweetwater River, both in Nebraska. Later versions of his life claimed he faced several perilous days as a Pony Express rider, including outrunning Lakota warriors on his mail horse and engaging in a shootout with a pair of trail bandits.

In his autobiography, Cody described how he had made a record-setting run one day in the summer of 1860. He had headed westward out of Red Buttes carrying the mail. His horse moved along at a fast gallop since the schedule required Cody to make the run averaging 15 miles per hour (24 kph).

On this particular day, when he reached the home station at Three Crossings after five hard hours on the trail, he discovered his replacement rider had been killed in a drunken fight the previous night. With no one to relieve him, young Cody returned to the trail after taking a meal served by the station supervisor's wife. He covered the next 72 miles (116 km) to Pacific Springs Station, which took him through South Pass in Wyoming. After 11 more hours in the saddle, he reached Pacific Springs. There was no replacement rider at Pacific Springs available to carry the eastbound mail, so he agreed to return to Red Buttes along the same trail, this time through the night. By the time he reached Red Buttes, he had ridden about 300 miles (480 km) in 22 hours, averaging close to 14 miles per hour (23 kph).

Cody was less than humble about his feat. He later remembered: "I pushed on with the usual rapidity, entering every relay station on

(continues)

(continued)

time, and accomplished the round trip to Red Buttes without a single mishap, on time."*** It is in the distance he claimed to have covered that controversy enters the picture. Cody stated that on that day he had covered a total distance of 384 miles (618 km), which would have been 4 miles longer than "Pony Bob" Haslam's record setter. As Cody himself stated: "This stands on the records as the longest Pony Express journey ever made."[†]

Is Buffalo Bill's claim of his record-setting distance ride true? Historians doubt it. Although historians disagree on the distance, claiming Cody's run fell somewhere between 296 miles and 388 miles (476 km and 624 km), the actual distance is closer to 300 miles (483 km). So, he may have been exaggerating. In addition, he did not claim to have made the longest ride for the Pony Express until he was the famous Buffalo Bill, who was not only a great showman, but also a self-promoter. (Not only do historians doubt the length of Cody's ride, some, including Louis S. Warren, doubt he was ever a Pony Express rider at all.)

---

* Louis S. Warren, *Buffalo Bill's America: William Cody and the Wild West Show* (New York: Alfred A. Knopf, 2005), 3.
** Ibid., 4.
*** Nevin, 105.
[†] Ibid.

(continued from page 101)

one of the riders who delivered the news of Lincoln's 1860 election, covering 75 miles (120 km) in just over four hours.

Fisher was so recognized for his skills and fortitude in the saddle that he was tapped to make another special ride in July 1860. With the Paiute on the warpath, he was to deliver the news from Ruby Valley through more than 300 miles (480 km) of hostile territory to the citizens of Salt Lake City. To avoid ambush, Fisher rode wide of the regular trail several times, yet completed his run in 34 hours. His message resulted in two U.S. Army companies being dispatched to Ruby Valley to make certain Pony Express riders were protected.

Others round out the legendary riders of the Pony Express. Some of those notables did not survive their service. Billy Tate rode the trail near Ruby Valley, Nevada, during a Paiute uprising. On a run, he was attacked by a group of American Indians and tried to outrun them on his horse. When he could not escape, he dismounted and tried to fight it out, taking shelter behind some large rocks. Before he was killed, he took the lives of seven of his attackers. His corpse was found bristling with arrows. He was not scalped, though, a sign that the Paiute thought he had defended himself with honor. What makes Tate's actions even more extraordinary is the fact that he was only 14 years old.

Men such as Warren Upson are remembered not for a singular exploit of dash and color, but for carrying the mail routinely through the High Sierra, often through snowstorms that hovered over the mountain for months out of the year. He repeatedly faced down blinding blizzards and pushed his horse along mountain trails through snowdrifts 30 feet (9 m) deep.

Then there was George Washington Thatcher, who told the story of one occasion when a wolf surprised his horse, sending him hurtling through the air. On foot, Thatcher managed to outrun the wolf, remount his pony, and ride out of harm's way.

Dozens of other riders are recalled for their daring and persistence while staring death in the face. But for every extraordinary hero of the Pony Express route, there were hundreds of riders and station keepers who kept to their routine and daily tasks, keeping up their efforts without note or recognition, to make certain the Pony Express completed its assigned task: to keep the nation's mail moving.

The Pony Express
at Trail's End

Even as newspapers ran exciting stories about the exploits of the Pony Express riders, turning the transcontinental line into the nation's most thrilling mail service, the financial story behind the service was bleak. William Russell—in all his excitement and determination to establish the line, and expecting a lucrative government contract once he proved his idea would work—had overspent in setting up his scheme. He had paid dearly or gone into debt deeply to pay top dollar for horses, relay stations, mail coaches for secondary lines, and good pay for the riders on whom he had risked his company and financial empire. Once the line opened, despite the thrills and adventures splashed across the daily and weekly papers, it would prove a drain. Russell and his colleagues lost close to $1,000 per day, and that elusive government contract never came through.

FINANCIAL WOES

There were additional sources of Russell's financial woes, as well. There had been other extensions of his company's reach across the West in 1860. He and his colleagues had hired thousands of men and purchased thousands of oxen to carry supplies to army posts. Then, at the last minute, Russell, Majors & Waddell realized another freighting company had underbid them for a significant portion of the delivery contracts they had been expecting to receive. For that portion of the contracts Russell and his associates did receive, the army proved slow in implementing them, dragging its heels in even giving Russell instructions about its needed delivery systems. In the meantime, the company had already hired workers and bought livestock. The hired hands needed to be paid and the oxen fed. Since the government did not pay until the deliveries were completed, Russell and his partners had to wait even longer than usual for compensation.

Everything seemed to be working against Russell, Majors & Waddell. With their freight, stage, and mail empires stretched to the limit with debt, the company began to feel a cash flow crunch. Months passed with Russell unable to make payroll. Workers for the company's Central Overland, California & Pike's Peak Express firm began to joke darkly about the company's inability to pay their wages, changing the meaning of the COC&PP's initials to read "Clean Out of Cash & Poor Pay."[1]

All this financial drama meant that Russell spent much of his time back East trying to drum up money for his company. When the army was slow to pay through the summer and fall of 1860, he even knocked on the door of Secretary of War John Floyd, more than once, demanding payment for services rendered. On one occasion, when Floyd did manage to pay Russell more than $160,000, the majority of those monies were sucked up by the company's huge debt service. Floyd even agreed to endorse credit extensions for Russell based on his future profits, to help Russell secure further loans. But nearly every banker he approached knew the story: The credit of Russell, Majors & Waddell was overextended, and only a fool would hand over money to the captain of a sinking ship.

Russell, his firm near economic ruin, was approached by a friend in the banking business, Luke Lea, who suggested he might get some help from a law clerk with the Department of the Interior, Godard Bailey. It seems Bailey was responsible for a pile of lucrative bonds the department held in trust, earmarked to support several western American Indian nations. Russell wasted no time making an appointment with Bailey. The clerk listened with interest to Russell's financial dilemma. When he was informed that Floyd had illegally supported and endorsed Russell's credit vouchers, he knew he had to give Russell what support he could. (If Secretary Floyd's actions had become public, he would have been criminally liable. As Bailey was married to Floyd's second cousin, the matter was partially a family issue.)

Bailey's support of Russell was simple, but illegal. The western entrepreneur would have access to American Indian bond monies, "loaned" to him by Bailey. He would use these as collateral to secure further bank loans, and then repay the bonds when the company was once again secure and making a profit. Much of this hinged on a future government contract for the Pony Express, which never came. In the meantime, Bailey would retain promissory notes written by Russell. This move was meant to secure the "loan" and, hopefully for Bailey, cover him legally if their private deal was exposed. With the credit vouchers in his hand, Bailey could argue that the monies were not "stolen," just borrowed. In fact, "the two men were indeed scrupulous about exchanging bonds and acceptances."[2] In all, Bailey provided $870,000 worth of bonds to Russell.

But the plans went awry. By December, the missing funds were discovered, and Bailey produced the vouchers Russell had signed. This did not mitigate his guilt or that of William Russell, who was arrested on December 24 in his New York office.

On the brink of financial ruin, William H. Russell turned to the secretary of war, John B. Floyd (*above*) for assistance. Floyd, however, soon had Russell and his partners in the Pony Express involved in a bonds scandal that landed Russell in jail.

Subsequently, he was charged with three counts of receiving stolen property and another charge of conspiring to defraud the government. Despite his fame and his other connections with the government through mail and coach contracts, Russell was taken to Washington, D.C., and placed in jail, his bail set at $500,000. As for Bailey, his role in the affair only brought him a $5,000 bail. A network of friends and business associates across the country paid Russell's bail after it was reset at $300,000.

UNDER INVESTIGATION

Not only did Russell face criminal charges, the House of Representatives began an investigation in January 1861, even as Southern states were beginning to secede from the Union. A House Select Committee held hearings through February, hearing the sworn testimony of 46 witnesses. Sometimes these witnesses contradicted one another. Russell testified in his defense four times, responding to questions with alternating frankness and confusion, claiming he did not remember dates or amounts of money in question.

By the time the committee finished its work and issued its report, Secretary Floyd had abandoned his government post and fled across the Potomac to Virginia, which would soon secede into the Confederacy. The committee concluded that Floyd had not only connived illegally with Russell and approved acceptances, but had done so with other businessmen, too. President Buchanan was also criticized for having been aware of Floyd's actions. Buchanan had told him to stop such activities, but had not followed up on the matter. Secretary of the Interior Jacob Thompson was also highly criticized and was considered guilty of neglect regarding the bonds that had been stolen. Bailey never stood for trial, dodging court summonses until the Civil War became the federal government's new focus.

As for William Russell, he managed to slip through the legal system on a technicality. His case went to criminal court in Washington in late January 1861, following his testimony before the House Select Committee. His lawyer brought to court a federal law, only three years old, that exempted congressional committee witnesses from being prosecuted criminally based on their earlier testimony. The judge could do little but dismiss Russell's case. Although Russell's day in court turned in his favor, he did not emerge from the scandal without personal and financial losses. Soon, he had no choice but to file for bankruptcy.

NEW ENTREPRENEURS

An ironic twist sealed the fate of Russell, Majors & Waddell. Even as the House Select Committee was holding hearings over the bonds scandal, Congress was meeting to discuss mail contracts for the new year. Debate centered on those supporting the central route, since the Pony Express had already proven the route's viability and its speed in delivering the mail. The House of Representatives voted in support of subsidizing the central route, passing a bill to that effect in February. Soon, word reached Washington that Confederate forces out West had cut off the Butterfield Overland Mail's stagecoach line, the route through the South that had served as a rival to the central route. This news pushed Congress to insist that Butterfield Overland Mail be switched to the central overland route, while at the same time eliminating competitive bidding for mail delivery along that line.

For John Butterfield and William Russell, the decision was a bitter pill. Just the previous year, Butterfield had been forced out of his own company for failing to pay company debts to its primary creditor, Wells, Fargo & Company. By February 1861, Wells Fargo was operating the Butterfield line. Transfer of Butterfield to the central route would place the line in direct competition with the COC and the Pony Express. Under the circumstances, and given the ongoing bonds scandal, the government would not begin to consider Russell and his associates in the new mail contract. Instead, the contract went to Wells, Fargo & Company, to the tune of $1 million annually.

This move by Congress crushed the future of the COC and Russell, Majors & Waddell. The tide was turning against them, the scandal only made everything worse, and "their known liabilities now exceeded their assets by around two million dollars and they had no choice but to go into bankruptcy."[3] Their freight wagon business dried up, ending an era.

Even as the company's viability ended, Russell knew it still had assets, including relay stations, stagecoaches, oxen and horses, and employees. The newly capitalized replacement of the Butterfield Line—Wells, Fargo & Company's Overland Mail Company—needed to operate all of this. Russell, unwilling to lie down and let his company completely collapse, turned a new trick. In March 1861, he handed over the western half of the COC's mail route to the Overland Mail Company, which should have meant little to the OMC at the time "since Congress had already awarded it the whole route."[4] But Overland accepted the offer, which gave Russell's COC the right to split the $1 million contract with the company that should have been its direct rival. Each company would operate its half of the Pony Express, providing government support for the line that had, to that date, been entirely funded by Russell and his associates.

Russell's coup would provide him little personal or professional gratification. The COC's creditors had lost faith in Russell and demanded that the presidency of the company be handed over to someone else. By April 26, 1861, Russell was forced to step down. In his place, officials chose a lawyer, Bela M. Hughes. Ironically, he was not only an old business friend of Russell's, one who had worked with Russell in earlier days in St. Joseph, but also a cousin of Ben Holladay, the head of a rival freighting company, who had been extending credit to the COC. Holladay therefore had a stake in the company's future.

To some, Holladay would really be pulling the strings, with Hughes as the front man. By March 1862, he called in the debts owed to him, which the COC could not possibly pay. Taking his case to court, Holladay received a court order to force the company to be sold at auction, where he bought it for a song—$100,000. The old guard of Russell, Majors, Waddell, and Butterfield were all but finished as entrepreneurs of the West. Their day had passed and a new era of transport across the West lay on the horizon—the advance of the railroad from coast to coast.

LATTER DAYS

Russell, Majors & Waddell had made a distinct impact on the American West, but the 1860s would provide their last hurrah. After his ousting as president of the COC, William Russell was no longer recognized as a mover and shaker on a national scale, nor were his two famous associates. Waddell managed to emerge from the company's bankruptcy, but the glory days were gone. He kept his mansion in Lexington, Missouri, only by selling it to his son for one dollar, while retaining the right to live there the remainder of his life.

Alexander Majors actually tried to keep his hand in the freighting business, cranking up a new freight company, but only lasted a few more years as he failed to make a viable profit. His decline continued as he floundered for direction. He continued to remain in the West and tried his hand at prospecting, but failed to make a strike. He faded out of public view and became a recluse, only to be rediscovered in his later years, destitute and "living alone in a shack near Denver, writing his memoirs of the frontier years."[5]

Perhaps ironically, the man who found the long forgotten entrepreneur was none other than Buffalo Bill Cody, whom Majors had employed as a Pony Express rider decades earlier. Cody tried to rescue Majors by paying for the former titan's memoirs to be published. They did not sell well, though, as the vast majority of Americans no longer remembered Majors. Those who did so did not recall him from his long years in the freighting business. They remembered him as one of the founders of the colorful Pony Express.

Perhaps none of the freighting trio sunk lower in forced retirement than William Russell. He tried to continue his reputation as an innovator of transportation systems through the West. He relied once again on his legendary personal and professional charm to lure backers, especially old friends, to put up monies for his latest schemes. Among them, Russell made plans to establish two road construction companies out in Colorado, one of his former stomping grounds.

His plans never saw reality. He moved to New York City, where he had maintained offices for years, and was accepted as a partner in a brokerage firm that sold mining stock in the West. Again, his business schemes failed, even costing him his New York City home located at 686 Broadway. Russell was so destitute that he was forced to write a letter to his old partner William Waddell, asking for $200 to pay for the expense of filing a legal petition for bankruptcy. Waddell gave him the money. At the end of his life he was selling Tic Sano, a patent medicine that claimed to treat the nerve disorder neuralgia. He died of a stroke in 1872.

The Pony Express did not remain in business more than six months after Russell was forced to step down as president of the COC in April 1861. The line never did manage to make money, and only cost Russell and his colleagues for each day it ran from Missouri to California.

Even though the finances of the Pony Express never worked out, the system was doomed anyway. It would be replaced by an even quicker method of delivering messages across the great expanses of the American West: the telegraph. Throughout the summer of 1861, crews were busy stringing telegraph poles and wire along the same route the Pony Express used to deliver the mail. As the telegraph moved across the Great Plains, the Pony Express shrunk. By late August, when electric lines had been strung nearly 100 miles

THE OVERLAND PONY EXPRESS.—[Photographed by Savage, Salt Lake City, from a Painting by George M. Ottinger.]

Although the riders and horses of the Pony Express were able to quickly deliver messages from one coast to the other, they were unable to keep up with the advances in technology. The invention of the telegraph was faster, safer, and cheaper, and the Pony Express was soon obsolete. Above, a Pony Express courier rides along his route while workers erect poles for telegraph lines.

(160 km) west of Nebraska's Fort Kearny, the horse and rider system no longer ran farther eastward. Telegraph stringing crews made fast progress delivering the telegraph to the East out of Carson City, Nevada, sometimes advancing the line as many as 25 miles (40 km) in a single day.

Finally, the telegraph reached Salt Lake City from both directions. The date was October 24, 1861. Before the end of the month, the first telegram was sent across the United States from West to East. This first transcontinental electric

(continues on page 118)

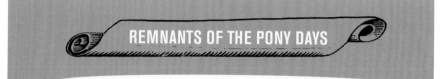

Although the Pony Express went out of business a century and a half ago, some of the old stations either still exist today or have been painstakingly reconstructed on or near their original locations. Modern-day tourists and history buffs might begin their exploration of the Pony Express route by visiting its original headquarters town of St. Joseph, Missouri. The reconstructed Patee House is a grand brick façade, standing four stories tall. In the Patee House, tourists may view the reconstructed offices of Russell, Majors & Waddell. The restored sites connected to the Pony Express in St. Joseph also include reconstructed stables, a completely furnished tack room, and a blacksmith shop.

The only original and unaltered Pony Express station in existence today is the Hollenberg Station, which stands in Hanover, Kansas. Compared to many Pony Express stations, the Hollenberg stop was substantial—an elongated clapboard structure with three front entrances. At other places along the route, such as Marysville, Kansas, towns have lovingly restored their Pony Express stations.

At Fairbury, Nebraska, the Rock Creek Station has been reconstructed as a special feature for visitors to the Rock Creek State Historical Park. Buildings include a substantial stable constructed out of vertically placed logs, and the East Ranch House and adjacent bunkhouse. A toll bridge that once spanned Rock Creek has also been rebuilt. At Nebraska's reconstructed Fort Kearny, visitors may view a stockade, blacksmith shop, and buildings constructed out of sod.

Gothenberg, Nebraska, is today home to two restored Pony Express stations, the Midway Station and Machette's (or Sam Mechette's) Station, which was moved to Gothenberg from its original location southwest of Brady, Nebraska. Originally a two-story log building, Machette's has only been restored to one story. At Cozad, Nebraska, the Willow Island Station has been restored and moved from its original site near Lexington. The Midway, Machette's, and Willow Island stations are all simple horizontal log cabins.

Some controversy exists today over whether Machette's was actually a Pony Express station, even though some sources indicate it was. At its original location, Machette's was situated just 5 miles (8 km) west of the Cottonwood Springs Station and about 8 miles (13 km) from Gilman's Station to the east, placing it too close to either to be a Pony Express stop. Unquestionably, Machette's was a stage-coach stop and its blacksmith shop may have been used by the Pony Express.

In Wyoming, an important Pony Express stop was Fort Laramie, which has been largely restored and includes a complex of fort-related buildings. At Granger, Wyoming, the old South Bend Stage Station remains, built of native rock. Ham's Fork Station stood nearby, as a mere dugout. Reconstructed buildings at the Fort Bridger State Historic Site offer visitors a look at the Pony Express station and trading post that existed a century and a half ago. Sites include the Pony Express stable and the sutler's store, where riders picked up and delivered the mail.

Utah's Camp Floyd Station, Carson's Inn, has been reconstructed as a two story, whitewashed building with front porches on both stories. Carson's Inn also served as a stagecoach stop. Out in the desert is the restored Simpsons Springs Station, located on Pony Express Byway just west of Faust, Utah. The old stagecoach and Pony Express road is still visible. Farther west of Faust, visitors may view the ruins of the rock-built Boyd's Station, also on Pony Express Byway.

Today, the remains of Nevada's Antelope Springs Station are nothing more than a pile of rocks and a scattering of log timbers. The Egan's Canyon Station also no longer stands, but nearby a primitive

(continues)

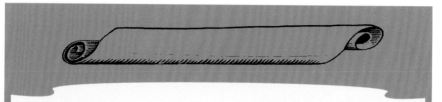

(continued)

cemetery does. The Ruby Valley Station, a basic vertical log construction, has been relocated to Elko, Nevada. Only the partial walls of the Diamond Springs Station remain, north of Eureka, Nevada, as well as the ruins of the Dry Creek Station, east of Austin. Low running stonewalls are all that remain today of the Cold Springs Station, east of Fallon. Southwest of Fallon, the stables and corrals of Buckland's Station still remain, as well as the ruined adobe walls of Fort Churchill. Located at Mormon Station State Historic Park is the reconstructed Genoa (or Old Mormon) Station, which includes the log cabin station, vertical log stockade, and rebuilt pony stables.

In California, the Pleasant Grove House (or Duroc) Station still remains, north of the town of Rescue. The two-story, white clapboard house was first built as an inn in 1850 and later became a Pony Express station. At Folsom, California, visitors may stop by the Wells Fargo Building, an assay office that dates to 1860. It served as the location of the Folsom Station. In California's state capital of Sacramento, the impressive Hastings Building, which housed the Wells Fargo office and the Sacramento Station, is a monument to the end of the Pony Express trail.

(continued from page 115)

missive was sent from California Chief Justice Stephen Field to Abraham Lincoln. In it, Field offered congratulations to the president on the completion of the telegraph line from coast to coast, and offered the support of California to the Union cause against the Confederate states in the Civil War.

With the completion of the cross-country telegraph line, the demise of the Pony Express seemed close at hand. Newspapers began running stories predicting how much longer the horse-run mail delivery system could remain in business. Everyone knew that Russell's scheme had always been a money loser. Interested parties crunched the Pony Express numbers and printed them in the press. By some calculations, during the Pony Express's first 18 months of operation, the mail system had delivered about 35,000 pieces of mail at a cost to the company of about $16 per piece. It had only received, on average, $3 per letter. This translated into net losses between the spring of 1860 and the fall of 1861 of $300,000 to $500,000, an amount equivalent to millions or even tens of million of dollars in today's money.

Although the completion of the transcontinental telegraph line heralded the limited future of the Pony Express, it did not immediately kill it off. Along various regional sections of the line, Pony Express riders continued to ride their mounts hard to deliver their mail pouches over short local runs. It seemed at times that the Pony Express riders were unwilling to admit their delivery system was no longer relevant. The last run took place on November 20, 1861, with the delivery of the mail to the Pony Express office in San Francisco. Almost immediately, that rider (whose name is not remembered) began looking for a new line of work.

Was the Pony Express a total failure? Certainly not. It is certain that the system never managed a profit, but it was a success in other ways. For one, at a time in U.S. history when the federal government needed proof that a central mail route was the most practical, the Pony Express offered proof. The trail used by the Pony Express would also serve as the basic route for the building of the first transcontinental railroad across the Great Plains and Inter-Mountain region during the mid to late 1860s. In addition, the legacy of the Pony Express would include tales of adventure and self-sacrifice by riders, which inspired generations of Americans to follow. It is certain that "the Pony [Express] had profited no one, but it had immeasurably enriched the whole country."[6]

Although obituaries for the Pony Express ran in dozens of U.S. newspapers, perhaps none provided greater tribute than an editorial featured on the pages of the California journal *Pacific*:

> A fast and faithful friend has the Pony [Express] been to our far-off state. Summer and winter, storm and shine, day and night, he had traveled like a weaver's shuttle back and forth til now his work is done. Goodbye, Pony! No proud and star-caparisoned charger in the war field has ever done so great, so true and so good a work as thine. No pampered and world-famed racer of the turf will ever win from you the proud fame of the fleet courser of the continent. You came to us with tidings that made your feet beautiful on the tops of the mountains; tidings of the world's great life, of nations rising for liberty and winning the day of battles, and nations defeats and reverses. We have looked to you as those who wait for the morning, and how seldom did you fail us! When days were months and hours weeks, how you thrilled us out of our pain and suspense, to know the best or now the worst. You served us well![7]

CHRONOLOGY

1847 U.S. Congress passes a bill approving the construction of five steamships to deliver the mail to the Pacific Coast. Western entrepreneur William Russell begins operating his first wagon freighting business.

1848 The Southwest, including California, becomes U.S. territory after Mexico's defeat in the Mexican-American War.

1849 A gold rush in Northern California causes tens of thousands of would-be prospectors to flood into the Pacific territory. That year, Henry O'Rielly suggests to Congress that a telegraph line be established across the West to California. The suggestion is rejected. Also, Alexander Majors takes his first wagon train to Santa Fe.

1850 California gains statehood. That same year, Woodward and Chorpenning sign a government contract to deliver the mail from Sacramento to Salt Lake City. Samuel Woodson signs a similar contract to deliver the mail between Salt Lake City and Independence, Missouri.

1852 O'Rielly suggests a system of riders and horses to deliver the mail across the West to California. Congress rejects the idea. That year, William Russell and William Waddell establish the freighting firm of Waddell & Russell.

1856 Russell, Majors & Waddell is established.

1858 U.S. government signs a contract with the Butterfield Overland Company to deliver mail via a stagecoach route across the Southwest to California.

1860 **January** Russell meets with congressmen to propose the Pony Express, and commits his company to the endeavor without a government contract.

April 3 The Pony Express begins its first run, sending riders with the mail from both the East and the West.

April 13 Two riders, one in the East and one in the West, complete the first run of the Pony Express.

May The Paiute War lasts the month, resulting in significant disruption to the infant Pony Express.

December Russell is arrested in New York, charged with conspiring to defraud the U.S. government.

1861   **January** House investigation begins into Russell's illegal receipt of American Indian trust monies from the Department of the Interior.

TIMELINE

1848
The Southwest, including California, becomes U.S. territory after Mexico's defeat in the Mexican-American War

1850
Woodward and Chorpenning sign a government contract to deliver the mail from Sacramento to Salt Lake City. Samuel Woodson signs a similar contract to deliver the mail between Salt Lake City and Independence, Mo.

1848   1856

1849
Alexander Majors takes his first wagon train to Santa Fe

1852
William Russell and William Waddell establish the freighting firm of Waddell & Russell

1856
Russell, Majors & Waddell is established

February Wells Fargo takes operating control of the Butterfield Stage Line.

March Russell transfers the western half of the COC's mail route to the Overland Mail Company (the old Butterfield Line) to gain government financial support for the Pony Express.

April Russell is ousted from the presidency of the COC by his creditors.

October 24 The transcontinental telegraph line reaches Salt Lake City from both East and West, rendering the Pony Express out of date.

November 20 The last run of the Pony Express takes place.

1858
U.S. government signs a contract with the Butterfield Overland Company to deliver mail via a stagecoach route across the Southwest to California

April 3, 1860
The Pony Express begins its first run

December 1860
Russell is arrested in New York, charged with conspiring to defraud the U.S. government

1858

1861

January 1860
Russell meets with congressmen to propose the Pony Express, and commits his company to the endeavor

April 13, 1860
Two riders, one in the East and one in the West, complete the first run of the Pony Express

February 1861
Wells Fargo takes operating control of the Butterfield Stage Line

NOTES

CHAPTER 1

1. David Nevin, *The Expressmen.* New York: Time-Life Books, 1974, 91.
2. Paul Robert Walker and Paul Robert, *True Tales of the Wild West.* Washington, D.C.: National Geographic, 2002, 61.
3. Ibid.
4. Joseph DiCerto, *The Saga of the Pony Express.* Missoula, MT: Mountain Press Publishing Company, 2002, 48.
5. Walker, 62.
6. Nevin, 92.
7. DiCerto, 49.
8. Nevin, 92.
9. Walker, 53.
10. Ibid.

CHAPTER 2

1. Nevin, 21.
2. Ibid., 24.
3. Ibid., 27.
4. Ibid.
5. Ibid., 31.
6. Ibid.
7. Ibid.
8. Ibid., 35.
9. Ibid., 32.
10. Ibid.
11. Ibid., 35.

CHAPTER 3

1. DiCerto, 28.
2. Nevin, 62.
3. DiCerto, 32.
4. Ibid.
5. Ibid.

CHAPTER 4

1. Nevin, 100.
2. DiCerto, 43.
3. Ibid.
4. Ibid.
5. Nevin, 101.
6. Christopher Corbett, *Orphans Preferred: The Twisted Truth and Lasting Legend of the Pony Express.* New York: Broadway Books, 2003, 84.
7. Walker, 65.
8. Ibid., 66.
9. Ibid., 68.
10. Ibid., 69.

CHAPTER 5

1. DiCerto, 71.
2. Ibid., 72.
3. Ibid., 77.
4. Ibid., 79.
5. Ibid., 80.
6. Ibid., 83.
7. Ibid., 86.
8. Ibid.
9. Corbett, 93.
10. Ibid., 86.
11. Ibid., 88.
12. Diane Yancey, *Life on the Pony Express.* San Diego: Lucent Books, 2001, 44.
13. Corbett, 81.
14. Ibid., 86.
15. Ibid., 87.

CHAPTER 6

1. Nevin, 117.
2. Ibid.

3. Fred Reinfeld, *Pony Express.* Lincoln: University of Nebraska Press, 1973, 54.

4. Nevin, 117.

5. DiCerto, 165.

6. Corbett, 88.

7. Ibid., 89.

8. Ibid.

9. Ibid., 90.

10. Ibid.

11. Ibid.

12. DiCerto, 96.

13. Ibid., 169.

14. Ibid., 170.

CHAPTER 7

1. Ibid., 180.

2. Ibid., 182.

3. Ibid.

CHAPTER 8

1. Ibid.

2. Ibid., 108.

3. Ibid., 110.

4. Ibid.

5. Ibid., 112.

6. Ibid., 113.

7. Ibid.

BIBLIOGRAPHY

Corbett, Christopher. *Orphans Preferred: The Twisted Truth and Lasting Legend of the Pony Express.* New York: Broadway Books, 2003.

DiCerto, Joseph. *The Saga of the Pony Express.* Missoula, Mont.: Mountain Press Publishing Company, 2002.

Ellis, Jerry. *Bareback!: One Man's Journey Along the Pony Express Trail.* New York: Delacorte Press, 1993.

Moeller, Bill and Jan. *The Pony Express: A Photographic History.* Missoula, Mont.: Mountain Press Publishing Company, 2002.

Nevin, David. *The Expressmen.* New York: Time-Life Books, 1974.

Rau, Margaret. *The Mail Must Go Through: The Story of The Pony Express.* Greensboro, N.C.: Morgan Reynolds Publishing, 2005.

Reinfeld, Fred. *Pony Express.* Lincoln: University of Nebraska Press, 1973.

Smith, Waddell F., ed. *The Story of the Pony Express.* San Francisco: Hesperian House, 1960.

Walker, Paul Robert. *True Tales of the Wild West.* Washington, D.C.: National Geographic, 2002.

Warren, Louis S. *Buffalo Bill's America: William Cody and the Wild West Show.* New York: Alfred A. Knopf, 2005.

Yancey, Diane. *Life on the Pony Express.* San Diego: Lucent Books, 2001.

WEB SITES

Fort Laramie National Historic Site

http://www.nps.gov/fola

This site is operated by the National Parks Service, which
supports and protects Fort Laramie, among other parks
and sites.

National Pony Express Association

http://www.xphomestation.com/npea.html

Chief supporter for the preservation of the Pony Express
National Historic Trail.

Pony Express Historical Association

http://www.stjoseph.net/ponyexpress

Pony Express National Museum

http://www.ponyexpress.org

National landmark Pony Express headquarters and owners
and operators of the Patee House Museum and Home of
Jesse James.

St. Joseph Museums

http://www.stjosephmuseum.org

This nonprofit organization encompasses Missouri's local muse-
ums dedicated to the research, preservation, interpretation,
exhibition, and teaching of St. Joseph and the Midland Empire's
history and cultures.

The Virtual Museum of the City of San Francisco: When the Pony Express Was in Vogue

http://www.sfmuseum.org/hist1/pxpress.html

A research and education site operated for scholars, featuring the
interesting, amusing, and unusual in San Francisco's history.

FURTHER READING

Fuchs, Bernie. *Ride Like the Wind: A Tale of the Pony Express.*
  New York: Scholastic, 2004.

Harness, Cheryl. *They're Off!: The Story of the Pony Express.*
  New York: Aladdin Paperbacks, 2002.

Jordan, Shirley. *Pony Express: Heroes in the Saddle.* Logan, Ia.:
  Perfection Learning Corporation, 2000.

Landau, Elaine. *The Pony Express.* New York: Scholastic
  Library Publishing, 2006.

Mercati, Cynthia. *The Pony Express.* Logan, Ia.: Perfection
  Learning Corporation, 2000.

Williams, Jean Kinney. *The Pony Express.* Mankato, Minn.:
  Coughlan Publishing, 2002.

WEB SITES

American West: Pony Express Information
http://www.americanwest.com/index2.htm
Site detailing the history and development of the American West
  and the Pony Express.

City of St. Joseph
http://www.ci.st-joseph.mo.us/history/ponyexpress.cfm
The history of St. Joseph and information on visiting the Pony
  Express Museum.

St. Joseph Convention and Visitor's Bureau
http://www.stjomo.com/
The history of St. Joseph, Missouri, the place of the Pony

Express Home Station and Jesse James.

FILMS

Cody of the Pony Express (1950)

Pony Express (1953)

Pony Express Rider (1976)

Winds of the Wasteland (1936)

The Young Riders (1989)

PHOTO CREDITS

INDEX

American Express Company, 25
American Indians
  attack on Woodward and
    Chorpenning, 21–22
  attacks on riders, 87, 98–99,
    105
  attacks on stations, 86–87, 89,
    98, 99
  Bayard proposal and, 27
  bonds for government sup-
    port of, 108, 110
  Butterfield Line and, 29
  Cody and, 102, 103
  section of route most often
    attacked, 57
Antelope Springs Station, 117
Apache, 27
Aspinwall, William H., 15

Bailey, Godard, 108
Bayard, W., 27–28
Bee, Frederick A., 32–33
Benicia Station, 91
Birch, James, 23
Boyd's Station, 117
"Bronco Charlie," 90–91
Brown, Aaron, 24, 25
Brown, James, 37
Buchanan, James, 110
Buckland's Station, 96, 99, 118
Buffalo Bill, 102–104, 113
Bullard, James H., 36
Burton, Sir Richard, 70
Butterfield, John, 25–26, 28–29,
  111
Butterfield Line, 25–26, 28–30
Butterfield Overland Mail Com-
  pany, 23, 111

Byram, Susan, 38

California (steamship), 15–16
Camp Floyd Station, 117
Campbell, William, 78, 81–83
cantinas (mail pockets), 4, 76
Cates, W.A., 4
Central America (steamship), 23
Central Overland California &
  Pike's Peak Express Company
  (COC&PP)
  established, 45
  horses, 46–47, 74–75
  route, 49, 64–70
  salaries, 50–51, 73, 81
  salaries, inability to pay, 107
  sale of western half of, 112
  stations, 46, 47–49
  See also specific stations
Chicago Tribune (newspaper), 24
Chorpenning, George, 19, 21–
  23, 45–46
Civil War, 2, 29–31, 111
Clark, Addison "Ad," 9–10
Cleve, Richard, 83, 85
Cliff, Charlie, 80
Cody, William Frederick, 102–
  104, 113
Cold Springs Station, 65, 98
collection sites, 52
communications, advances in, 2
  See also telegraph
Corbett, Christopher, 71
costs
  bonuses, 99
  Butterfield Line, 25
  daily losses, 106
  horses, 46

Jackass Line, 24
per piece of mail, 53, 75, 77,
   119
profitability and, 106–107,
   119
salaries, 50–51, 73, 81
salaries, inability to pay, 107
steamship, 16
Woodson, 18
Woodward and Chorpenning,
   21, 22–23
Cottonwood Springs Station,
   117

Davis, George H., 9
Deep Creek Station, 86
Diamond Springs Station, 118
Dry Creek Station, 118
Duroc Station, 118

Egan, Howard, 22, 57
Egan's Canyon Station, 117–118
Egan's Trail, 22
express stations, 70

Ficklin, Benjamin F., 32, 47
Field, Stephen, 118
Fisher, Billy, 101, 104–105
Floyd, John, 107, 108, 110
Folsom Station, 118
Fort Kearny
   Cleve and, 83
   on Pony Express route, 65
   reconstructed, 116
freighting companies
   Majors, 40, 42–43
   Majors and Russell, 102
   Russell, Bullard and McCarty,
      36
   Russell, Majors & Waddell,
      7, 33, 35, 37, 40–41, 44,
      106–107
   Russell and Brown, 37

Waddell & Russell, 37, 38
Fry(e), Johnny
   background of, 71
   eastbound mail and, 60
   opening day ride of, 8, 10–11,
      53–54
   women admirers of, 79

Genghis Khan, 31
Giddings, George, 23
The Gilded Age (Twain), 5
Gilman's Station, 117
"Great Register of the Desert,"
   67
Gull, James, 35–36
Gwin, William M., 32, 33

Hamilton, William, 55, 60–62
Hannibal & St. Joseph Railroad,
   7, 9–10
Harris, Arnold, 15
Haslam, Robert, "Pony Bob,"
   95–96, 98–101, 104
Haywood, J.T.K., 9
Hockaday Stage Line, 45
Holladay, Ben, 112–113
Hollenberg Station, 116
home stops, 47, 49
horse relay system
   early advocates of, 32–33
   historic, 31
   Russell and, 3–4, 33, 35
horses
   care of, 47
   changing, 47, 74–75
   distance covered by indi-
      vidual, 3
   purchased for Pony Express,
      46–47
"the horseshoe" route, 24
House of Representatives Select
   Committee, 110, 111
Hughes, Bela M., 112

Independence Rock, 66–67
Indians. *See* American Indians
Inman, Henry, 76–77

Jackass Line, 23–24
James, William, 94
Jones, John, 46
Julesburg Station, 95
jumping-off locations
    San Francisco, California, 1,
        16, 55, 69–70
    St. Joseph, Missouri, 1, 4, 5,
        7–8, 64, 116

Kearny, S.W., 37
Keetley, Jack, 93–94
Kiowa Station, 85

Landis, Israel, 4
Lea, Luke, 108
Leavenworth Daily Times (news-
    paper), 49
legacy of Pony Express, 119–120
Little, Feramorz, 19

Machette's Station, 116, 117
mail delivery in East, 13–14
mail delivery systems
    historic, 31
    horse relay system advocates,
        32–33
    Russell and, 3–4, 33, 35
mail delivery to West
    advocates for Pony Express,
        3–4, 32–33
    last by Pony Express, 119
    number of pieces delivered
        by Pony Express, 77–78, 119
    by ocean before Pony
        Express, 2–3, 13, 15–17
    overland before Pony Express,
        2–3, 19–26, 28–30
    route of Pony Express, 2, 49,

52, 64–70
    types of mail carried by Pony
        Express, 75
mail stations. See stations
Majors, Alexander
    background of, 38–40
    bankruptcy of Russell, Majors
        & Waddell and, 113–114
    Campbell and, 82
    horse relay system and, 35
    opening day speech by, 7–8
    religion and, 42–43
Majors, Benjamin, 39
Majors and Russell, 102
Marley, W.C., 98, 99
McCarty, E.C., 36
Mexico, 12–13
Middlegate Station, 99
Midway Station
    Cleve and, 83
    Moore and, 94–95
    position on route, 65
    restored, 116, 117
Miller, Charlie, "Bronco Char-
    lie," 90–91
Missouri (locomotive), 9–10
mochilas (saddle kits), 4–5, 10,
    76–77
Modoc, 100
Moore, Jim, 94–95

Native Americans. See American
    Indians
Neece, Peter, 86
New York Post (newspaper), 29
nickname, 63
Numaga (Paiute chief), 59

ocean mail routes, 2–3, 13,
    15–17
Old River Station, 98
opening day
    ceremonies, 4, 5, 7–8

eastbound departure, 1, 55
first riders, 55
overdue mail train, 9–10
westbound departure, 53
Oregon Trail, 18–19
Oregon Trail (old), 49, 65
O'Reilly, Henry, 31–32
Orphans Preferred (Corbett), 71
overland mail routes
    Butterfield Line, 25–26,
      28–30
    Civil War and, 111
    historic, 31
    Hockaday Stage Line, 45
    map, 20
    Pony Express, 2, 49, 52, 64–70
    Woodson, 18–19
    Woodward and Chorpenning,
      19, 21–23, 45–46
"the oxbow route," 24

Pacific (journal), 120
Pacific Mail Steamship Com-
  pany, 15
Paiute
    attacks by, 96, 98, 99
    proposed route and, 2
Paiute War, 58–59
Patee House, 116
Persian Empire, 31
Pioneer Trail, 49
Placerville Station, 91
Platte River, 65–66
Pleasant Grove House Station,
  118
Polk, James K., 13
"The Pony," 63
profitability of Pony Express,
  106–107, 119
Pyramid Lake Massacre, 58

railroads
    first to cross Missouri, 7

Pony Express and, 7, 9–10
Randall, James, 8–9, 55
Reed's Station, 96
relay system of mail delivery,
  background of, 31–33
Richardson, Billy, 8, 55
Richardson, Johnny, 98
riders
    attacks by American Indians,
      57, 87, 98–99, 105
    attacks by thieves, 74
    bonuses, 99
    characteristics of, 71, 73
    dangers from animals, 55–57,
      82
    distance covered on single
      mount, 74
    first eastbound, 8–9, 55–57,
      55–66
    first westbound, 8, 10–11,
      53–54, 55, 57–58, 60–62
    as heroes, 63, 79, 80–81
    hiring, 49–50
    last surviving, 91
    rugged terrain endured by,
      66, 68, 69
    salaries, 50, 73, 81
    station conditions endured
      by, 70–71
    time in saddle without relief,
      75, 83
    time spent at stations by, 3
    weather conditions endured
      by, 19, 21, 56–57, 58, 64, 68,
      82, 85–86, 101
    youngest, 90–91, 105
    See also specific individuals
Ringo, Samuel, 35–36
Rising, Don, 54
"road agents," 74
Rock Creek Station, 116
Roughing It (Twain), 71
Ruby Valley Station, 118

Russell, Majors & Waddell
   American Indian bonds and,
     108, 110
   bankruptcy, 113–114
   change in leadership, 112–
     113
   credit of, 108
   established, 37, 44
   as freighting company, 7, 33,
     35, 37, 40–41, 44, 106–107
   profitability of, 106–107, 112,
     119
Russell, William H.
   background of, 35–37
   bankruptcy of Russell, Majors
     & Waddell and, 114
   choice of St. Joseph as jump-
     ing-off point, 7
   criminal charges against,
     110–111
   financial problems, 106–108,
     111
   loss of presidency, 112
   mail delivery system pro-
     posed by, 3–4, 33, 35
   opening day speech by, 7

Sacramento, California, 69–70,
   118
Sacramento Union (newspaper),
   24
saddle kits, 4–5, 76–77
Salt Lake City, 18–19, 21, 22, 57,
   68
San Francisco, California
   delivery beyond, 69–70
   on first day of Pony Express,
     1
   mail delivery to, before Pony
     Express, 16
   opening day, 55
Sand Springs Station, 99
Seventy Years on the Frontier

(Majors), 43
Shell Creek Station, 86
Simpson, James, 69
Simpson Route, 69
Sink of Carson Station, 98, 99
Slade, Joseph, 71
Sloo, A.G., 15
Smith's Creek Station, 96, 98
South Bend Station, 117
speed
   Butterfield Line, 26
   first deliveries, 60
   importance of, 74
   importance of horses', 47
   mail delivery before Pony
     Express, 16–17
Sportsman's Hall Station, 91
St. Joseph, Missouri
   characteristics of, 64
   on opening day of Pony
     Express, 1, 4, 5, 7–8
   original Pony Express head-
     quarters, 116
   reasons chosen as jumping-
     off point, 7
St. Joseph Weekly (newspaper),
   52
stagecoaches
   Butterfield Line, 25–26, 28
   in Eastern U.S., 14
   road building proposal for,
     27–28
   Wells Fargo & Company, 101
stations
   attacked by American Indi-
     ans, 86–87, 89, 98, 99
   COC&PP, 46, 47–49
   currently, 116–118
   distance between, 3
   Paiute War and, 59
   relay system of Genghis
     Khan, 31
   time riders spent at, 3

types of, 47, 70–71
See also specific stations
steamships, 13, 14, 15–17
swing stops, 47, 49

Tabby (American Indian), 87–88
Tate, Billy, 90, 105
technology, advances in, 2
telegraph
    early proposals for transcontinental, 31–32
    messages carried by Pony Express, 53, 75
    as replacement for Pony Express, 114–115, 118–119
Thatcher, George Washington, 55–57
thieves, 74
Thompson, Jacob, 110
Thompson, Meriwether Jeff, 5, 7
tourism, 116–118
transportation
    advances in, 2
    in Eastern U.S., 14
    railroads, 7, 9–10
    road building proposal, 27–28
    stagecoaches, 14, 25–26, 28, 101
    in Western U.S., 18
Twain, Mark
    basis for character in *Roughing It*, 71
    basis for character in *The Gilded Age*, 5
    on Pony Express riders, 73, 80

Upson, Warren, 55–57, 105
U.S. Congress
    Butterfield Line and, 23
    financial support of Pony Express, 53

House Select Committee, 110, 111
    money for building roads and, 27–28
    role in mail delivery, 14–15
    Woodson and, 18
    Woodward and Chorpenning and, 19, 21

Waddell, William B.
    background of, 37–38
    bankruptcy of Russell, Majors & Waddell and, 113, 114
    horse relay system and, 35
Waddell & Russell, 37, 38
Warder, Harriet Elliot, 36
Warren, Louis S., 104
weapons, 73
weather conditions, 64
    heat, 68
    rain, 58
    snow, 19, 21, 56–57, 83, 85–86, 101
The Weekly West (newspaper), 4, 8
weight
    of riders, 71, 73
    of saddles and kits, 4, 73, 76, 77
Weller, James B., 23
Wells Fargo & Company
    Butterfield Line and, 23, 112
    express riders for, 100
    sale of western half of COC&PP to, 112
    stagecoaches, 101
Western United States
    advocates for Pony Express, 3–4, 32–33
    expansion across, 12–13
    last mail delivery by Pony Express, 119

number of pieces of mail
   delivered by Pony Express,
   77–78, 119
ocean mail routes before
   Pony Express, 2–3, 13,
   15–17
overland mail routes before
   Pony Express, 2–3, 19–26,
   28–30
route of Pony Express, 2, 49,
   52, 64–70
transportation in, 18

types of mail carried by Pony
   Express, 75
Westgate Station, 99
Willow Creek Station, 86
Willow Island Station, 116–117
Wilson, Nick, 73, 74, 77, 85–92
Winnemucca (Paiute chief), 96
Woodson, Samuel H., 18–19
Woodward, Absalom, 19, 21–22

Young, Brigham, 19

About the Author

TIM McNEESE lives on a cutoff route of the Oregon Trail where he is associate professor of history at York College in York, Nebraska. He is in his seventeenth year of college instruction. McNeese earned an associate of arts degree from York College, a bachelor of arts in history and political science from Harding University, and a master of arts in history from Missouri State University. A prolific author of books for elementary, middle and high school, and college readers, McNeese has published more than 90 books and educational materials over the past 20 years, on everything from the civil rights movement to Spanish painters. His writing has earned him a citation in the library reference work *Contemporary Authors*, and multiple citations in *Best Books for Young Teen Readers*. In 2006, McNeese appeared on the History Channel program *Risk Takers, History Makers: John Wesley Powell and the Grand Canyon*. He was a faculty member at the 2006 Tony Hillerman Writers Conference in Albuquerque, where he lectured on the American Indians of the Southwest. McNeese and his wife, Beverly, sponsored study trips for college students on the Lewis and Clark Trail in 2003 and 2005 and to the American Southwest in 2008. Feel free to contact Professor McNeese at tdmcneese@york.edu.